Teaching for Transformation

Teaching from the Heart

Michel N. Christophe

Teaching for Transformation
Copyright © 2016. Michel N. Christophe

ISBN-13: 978-0-9987045-4-8
ProficiencyPlus

Contents

Chapter 1

BRIEFING OR TRAINING

Many people do a great job of briefing. Because their goal is simply to inform, briefing is really all they need to do. They are organized, knowledgeable, often charismatic, and in control of their performance. Briefing is a valuable skill, essential for the rapid dissemination of significant information. In industry, government, and many institutions of higher learning, briefing is what passes for training, and adult students have come to expect it.

When you expect people to retain, understand, and act on information you provide however, you have to do more than just deliver a message. You have to make sure listeners understand the message the way you intended it to be understood. To that end, it helps if you can get inside the listeners' heads. And you cannot do that unless you are able to get past concerns over your own performance, place the focus rightfully on the audience, and focus on the dynamics at play in the audience.

What is often missing from what passes for training in the form of briefings is an interest in drawing out listeners, an interest in actively connecting listeners to the issues under discussion in a way that is personal and spurs them on to contribute to and shape the event.

"People need to weigh in before they can buy in." The intention to cause an audience to negotiate meaning, feel something, react openly, argue constructively, and cause the contemplation of concepts to linger is associated with teachers, not briefers.

Logic, of course, should play a prominent role whenever people articulate ideas. Logic establishes relevance and competence. A necessary emotional connection, however, must be elicited, as it is responsible for creating the link that personalizes the learning experience. Making the topic of discussion personally relatable and actionable requires more than just a logical presentation of factual information. It requires that emotional connection. A change happens in the knowledge structure of participants as they engage each other and the teacher in an interactive exploration of the material. The emotional connection moves people to enrolment, ownership, and ultimately to action. It is only when we connect with people that we get them to see what we really want them to see.

A learning event is a cooperative effort between students and instructors. They feed off of one another. It is a social experience that like all successful social transactions requires a positive atmosphere. Effective teachers must be responsive to the students in their class. Good teaching is as much about passion as it is about reason. It's about not only motivating students to learn, but also teaching them how to learn...

It is about caring for your craft, having a passion for it, and conveying that passion to everyone, most importantly to your students. Good teaching is about substance [...] it's about doing your best to stay on top of your field ... bridging the gap between theory and practice. It's about listening, questioning, being responsive, and remembering that each student is different. It's about caring, nurturing, and developing minds and talents. It is also about having fun and basking in the rewards that learning brings.

One cannot learn to teach by reading a book, but reading a book can be an important step in a reflection that promotes better teaching and learning. Action that is not informed by reflection runs the risk of leading to diminishing returns. Through this book we aim to engage you, the reader, in a salutary reflection on ways to advance the concept of developing others. The scope of this endeavor goes beyond pedagogy and embraces leadership. Teaching is leadership in action. Teaching is enhanced when teachers are strong visionary leaders. We consider teaching an end within itself; real teachers love the art so much that it often becomes its own reward. Yet we also consider teaching to be a means and a pathway in the pursuit of transcendence, our own and that of those we touch. Frequent reflection, given the stakes, can only make the journey more rewarding.

The Banking Concept of Education [*Pedagogy of the Oppressed*]

When briefing passes for training, we are reminded of Paolo Freire's banking model of education. In this framework the ability to recall and regurgitate facts from class is the way to success. Education becomes an act of depositing, in which the students are the receptacles, the depositories and the teacher the depositor. In the banking concept of education knowledge is a gift bestowed by those who consider themselves knowledgeable upon those they consider to know nothing. The teacher presents himself to his students as their necessary opposites. The banking concept of education stimulates practices that mirror the practices of an oppressive society:

a) The teacher teaches and the students are taught;
b) The teacher knows everything and the students know nothing
c) The teacher thinks and the students are thought about
d) The teacher talks and the students listen – meekly
e) The teacher disciplines and the students are disciplined
f) The teacher chooses and enforces his choice, and the students comply
g) The teacher acts and the students have the illusion of acting through the action of the teacher

h) The teacher chooses the program content, and the students (who were not consulted) adapt to it
i) The teacher confuses the authority of knowledge with his or her own professional authority, which he or she sets in opposition to the freedom of the students
j) The teacher is the Subject of the learning process, while the students are mere objects

This banking concept smacks of education as an exercise in domination. Banking education begins with a false understanding of men and women as objects.

The Performance Model of education [*Pedagogy of the Distressed*]

Today we have class discussions, oral reports, and student participation of various kinds. The banking model should be obsolete. But according to Jane Tompkins, what we do have is something no less coercive, no less destructive of creativity and self-motivated learning. That something can be called the performance model.

While teachers believe they are helping students understand the material they are studying, what teachers are actually concerned with and focused on most of the time are three things:

a) To show the students how smart they are

b) To show the students how knowledgeable the teacher is, and
c) To show the students how well prepared the teacher is for class.

Teachers put on a performance whose true goal is not to help the students learn but to go through the motion and perform before them in such a way that students end up having a good opinion of the teacher.

This essentially, and more than anything else, is what we teach our students: how to perform within an institutional setting in such a way that they will be thought highly of by their colleagues and instructors.

How did it come to be that our main goal as instructors turned out to be performance?

Here is how Tompkins, who identified this model, answers the question:

"Each person comes into a professional situation dragging along behind her a long bag full of desires, fears, expectations, needs, resentments - the list goes on. But the main component is fear. Fear is the driving force behind the performance model. Fear of being shown up for what you are: a fraud, stupid, ignorant, a clod, a dolt, a sap, a weakling, someone who can't cut the mustard [...] Such fear is no doubt fostered by the way our institution is organized, but it is rooted in childhood [...] Fear of exposure, of being found out, does not have its basis in any real inadequacies either of knowledge or intelligence on our part, but rather in the performance model itself, which, in separating our behavior from what we really felt, created a kind of false self [...] We became so good at imitating the behavior of our elders, such expert practitioners at imitating whatever style, stance, or attitude seemed most likely to succeed in the adult world from which we so desperately sought approval that we came to be split into two parts: the real backstage self who didn't know anything and the performing self who got others to believe in its expertise and accomplishments. This pattern of seeking approval has extended itself into our practice as teachers. Still seeking approval from our peers and from our students, we exemplify a model of performance which our students succeed in emulating, thus passing the model down to future generations. Ironically, as teachers we are still performing for the teachers who taught us."

Education needs to become the practice of freedom, our own and that of our students.

Problem posing, Inquiry, critical thinking and dialogue are the tools of education for freedom. The voices of the learners inform the learning experience.

Dialogue:

To put it simply means, "to get it all out there"; it is a special type of discourse, which comes before decision-making. Debate is about winning, whereas dialogue is about learning.

Dialogue is about learning	Debate is about winning
Assuming that others have a piece of the answer	Assuming there is one right answer and you have it
Collaborative: looking for common understanding	Combative: attempting to prove the other side wrong
About finding common ground	About winning
Listening to understand and find basis for agreement	Listening to find flaws and make counterarguments
Bringing up your assumptions for inspection and discussion	Defending your assumptions
Discovering new possibilities and opportunities	Seeking an outcome that agrees with your position

Inquiry:
Any process that has the aim of augmenting knowledge, resolving doubt, or solving a problem.

Students and teachers must become partners in critical thinking. Teachers should replace banking educational goals with "the posing of the problems of human beings in their relations with the world". When students are given problems as opposed to only information, the process of learning becomes less alienating and more practical. When there is no one right answer, students are then pitted with the task of critical thinking.

1. What differentiates your training from a briefing?

2. What can you do to further differentiate your training from a briefing?

3. Where is your focus, on the subject, on the students, or on yourself?

4. How does your focus impact the learning experience?

Chapter 2

TEACHING WHO WE ARE

We teach who we are! What we learn well changes us. It changes our behavior, our skill set, and our awareness. We manipulate and process information before it sits in our memory, transforms and becomes knowledge. What we learn becomes us. Whenever we impart that knowledge to others, we teach them something that has become a part of the definition of who we are, something that made us who we are. Learning, when defined as a change in knowledge, behavior and attitude brought about by an experience, signals that what we have become reflects what we have learned. A musician, therefore, is clearly someone who has learned to play music. Learning is supposed to transform our thinking, our behaviors, and attitudes, and if it does not, it needs corrective attention. Ideally, by the time we are able to clearly articulate the concepts we intend to teach, we have presumably processed them so much that we understand them just as well as we can explain them. We have achieved mastery of some sort. We can extrapolate, see implications, make connections, and articulate what is essential about the concepts. What we know well and what we teach well becomes part of the definition of who we are.

We are the product of our connections. We learn through interactions with our peers and the physical world. Without connectedness, our learning stalls. The experiences we have had, what matters to us, what we want, who and what we love, who we focus on, all helps define who and what we are, as well as what we stand for. That is the stuff that makes us relatable. It provides a context to be tapped into ever so carefully. Teaching who we are and teaching from the heart become one and the same thing when our intimate familiarity with a concept unburdens us from relying on props as we elaborate on it. Teaching from the heart requires us to draw on information that resonates deeply with us and share it candidly. Teaching from the heart has direct implications for delivery, listeners' buy-in, listeners' enrolment and our ability to move others. Our teaching appears more authentic, more believable, more fluid, and less contrived. We show up in the classroom as real, feeling human beings, not drones regurgitating information.

When we teach who we are, we can relax and appear relaxed, which goes a long way in boosting our charisma. We can play up our natural warmth creating a feeling of intimacy that, in turn, makes opening up easier for an audience. We can have a heart-to-heart talk and leverage sincere feelings. When we teach from the heart, we exercise influence to a degree unparalleled with any other style of instruction. It never hurts to review and rehearse the material, which makes our performance appear even more effortless and natural.

When we teach from the heart, we talk straight, create transparency, confront reality, become accountable, and extend trust. We set the context for change and model the behavior that we expect. Teaching who we are can only be done credibly if we can take our knowledge of the subject matter in new directions, elaborate, simplify, expand, and summarize at will. We then will have captured the essence of our subject and can leverage our own experience to add to the scholarship in that domain. We have in effect become the main material of the class. Handbooks and slides are only props.

When we teach from the heart, our purpose is no longer simply to deliver a message; it is to spur people on to action. We want people to do something with the knowledge they are acquiring. When we teach from the heart we leverage the power of emotions. Emotions set people in motion. "Emotion" says Doug Stevenson, master storyteller, "is the fast lane to the brain." John Medina, the author of *Brain Rules* further validates Stevenson's point, saying, *"Emotionally charged events persist much longer in our memories and are recalled with greater accuracy than neutral memories."*

When we teach and speak from the heart, it becomes evident that we care. The audience experiences our emotions and we stimulate their interest at a primal level. We become totally plugged in emotionally, driven by unmitigated passion.

When, to illustrate a major point, we use stories that build on the point, have fun, and stimulate the imagination of our audience, our message sticks more. Doug Stevenson, a master storyteller, explains that stories are our most powerful tool for creating rapport. He invites us to find the lessons we learned in our stories of adversity, and then unleash them on the audience. Stevenson advises that to speak from the heart, we must tell the truth, and be honest with the audience; we must stand in our power, love ourselves, and let the audience watch; we must speak from our head with our heart wide open; tell people what we think and how we feel; and speak to them like they are our friends, rather than just as members of an audience.

To teach from the heart we have to have something significant to say, something we believe needs to be known, and something in which to be confident. Knowledge that absorbs our consciousness, and in the process, absolves us from the burden of self-consciousness can be taught from the heart. That compelling truth will be the source of the confidence we will feel and demonstrate. The knowledge will become us as we become it, at least in the eyes of the beholders. Having a mind filled with meaningful things to draw on and impart to others makes the fear of speaking in front of a group fade away. Teaching who we are is not an act of egotism or vanity. It is the highest expression of communion with the knowledge we share. It is a gift of self for the purpose of another's higher learning. It is an act of love.

Moving from the Concrete to the Abstract with the Triad Framework:

Ego, Environment and Wider World

To become meaningful, information needs to be personalized, made relatable, made to speak to us, and must be relevant to our needs. We need a connection. Learners benefit when information is articulated in very concrete ways; and abstractions are made concrete. Students do better when able to discuss how a piece of information relates to their personal life. They also need to be able to relate that same piece of information to their immediate environment, to the context in which they live, and to the wider world. This process seals the learning, moving from the self, to the immediate environment, to the larger world, from the concrete to the abstract, from the simple to the complex, every step of the way. This process of identifying the ramifications and implications of any idea to the self, the immediate environment and the larger world, causes concepts to resonate, to be understood, and to be articulated in ways that solidify learning and show integration.

Imagine a language learner confronted with having to reuse vocabulary she just learned. Imagine, especially if you have ever had to learn a foreign language, the level of effort that each step in the articulation of her narrative would require. Starting with the self, then moving to the immediate environment, and then moving to the wider world and drawing implications.

The more language is produced, the further away from self the narrative evolves, the more complex the thoughts and structures used become out of sheer linguistic necessity. People are always interested in relating whatever content they are learning to their lives and their very real need to communicate. People's urge to know and be known accelerates their language acquisition. With that approach, they feel as if they can immediately produce and use language that is relevant and compelling. Teach a new lesson with a focus on how each student can immediately reuse and integrate the information, or vocabulary shared, to talk about and describe their personal experiences moving each time from the concrete to the abstract, which makes their speech acts more complex. The self is the starting point of all new learning. It should also be the end point. All learning is ultimately learning about self. A strong emotional connection anchors the points.

With subjects other than foreign languages, such as leadership, the opposite approach is helpful: starting from the big picture, the worldview, and proceeding to the particular, the subjective, and the concrete ways in which the learner is affected by the object of study. In other words, one should bring the topic home to the student so it stops being some detached object of study. Have students answer the necessary question: what does this mean to you?

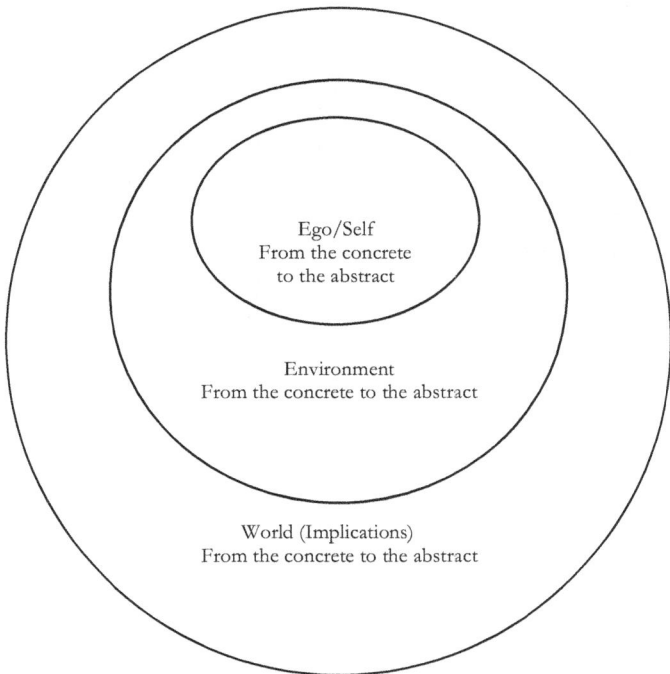

Ego/Self
From the concrete
to the abstract

Environment
From the concrete to the abstract

World (Implications)
From the concrete to the abstract

When teachers have students tactically relate newly covered information to their lives, and discuss it, teachers help students learn. People cannot be treated like sheep and expected to detach their personal reality from the context of learning. Students are central to the learning. At a minimum, we are teaching because they are there to learn. All learning becomes us.

You "teach who you are" when the subject that you teach is so ingrained in you that your behavior, attitudes, reflexes, and ways of thinking reflect a deep integration of the lessons you teach. You live and breathe that stuff!

What is learning anyway? Learning is intellectual, social, and emotional. It is ordered and it is erratic. It happens by design, and it happens by chance. It can be conscious and even unconscious. It is not limited to schools or formal classrooms. We all do it, even though we do not always have a clear sense of how it is happening or that it is happening at all.

There is no real consensus on the answer to the question, 'what is learning?' however, learning theorists – the behaviorists, the cognitivists, and more recently, the constructivists – have concocted learning theories which taken together give us a pretty good holistic sense of what learning is.

Behaviorism focuses only on the objectively observable aspects of learning. Behaviorists define learning as a change in behavior brought about by experience, with little concern for the mental or internal aspects of learning. Cognitive theories look beyond behavior to explain brain-based learning.

Cognitivists view learning as an active mental process of acquiring, remembering, and using knowledge. Cognitive learning is about enabling people to use their reason, intuition, and perception to learn. The cognitive view sees people as active learners who initiate experiences, seek out information to solve problems, and reorganize what they already know to achieve new insights. In fact, learning, within this perspective is seen as "transforming significant understanding we already have, rather than simple acquisitions written on blank slates." Learning is concerned with the acquisition of information about the environment, and with the acquisition of problem-solving skills with intelligence and conscious thought.

Constructivism views learning as a process in which the learner actively constructs new ideas or concepts. Constructivist perspectives on learning and teaching are increasingly influential today. These views are grounded in the psychological research of Piaget, Lev Vygotsky, Gestalt psychologists, Frederic Bartlett and Bruner, as well as the progressive educational philosophy of Dewey. Some constructivist views emphasize the shared, social construction of knowledge; others see social forces as less important. There is not just one constructivist theory of learning, but most of them agree on two central ideas:

> Learners are active in constructing their own knowledge.

> Social interactions are important in this knowledge construction process.

For our purpose here, our working definition of learning is: learning is a process through which experience causes permanent change in knowledge, attitude, and/or behavior.

Learning is about change. Learning is change. The change can be provoked, intentional, and for better or worse! To qualify as learning this change must be brought about by experience – by the interaction of a person with his or her environment.

1. How do you learn best?

2. What have you learned that has become essential to who you are today?

3. What is it that you expect students to do differently as a result of your instruction?

Chapter 3

TRAINING WITH
THE BRAIN IN MIND

The brain is involved in all aspects of the learning process. It is the single organ that is the central processor of all learning activities.

The concept of Whole Brain® Teaching and Learning is based upon a distribution of specialized modes throughout the brain system.

The model that has been developed divides the brain into four separate quadrants, each one different and equal in importance.

Two of these quadrants represent the more cognitive, intellectual modes (A and D), associated with the two upper cerebral hemispheres.

The other two quadrants (B and C) represent the more visceral, emotional modes associated with the lower limbic system.

The two left quadrants are specialized in left-mode thinking processes: logical, analytic, quantitative and fact based modes in the Upper Left A quadrant, and the more planned, organized, detailed and sequential mode processed in the Lower Left B quadrant.

In contrast, the other two right quadrants make up right-mode specialization: more synthesizing, integrating, holistic, and intuitive modes, the Upper Right D quadrant and the interpersonal, emotional, kinesthetic and feeling modes associated with the Lower Right C quadrant.

Fortunately, we are not limited to a one-quadrant perspective, but are "hard wired to be whole." There is "wiring" that crosses the center of our brain connecting the upper quadrants together and lower quadrants together.

The most successful approach to learning, design, and delivery is to create a "whole brain®" experience for a "composite whole brain®" learning group. This is accomplished by creating a "tapestry" of approaches, moving back and forth with techniques and activities from each of the four quadrants. Each key learning point, those that you "die" for, needs to be "paraphrased" in each mode at some point in the learning process. Using a Whole Brain® approach in your design and delivery helps insure that participants with different preferences and interests are able to learn effectively and consistently.

The Whole Brain® Thinking Model

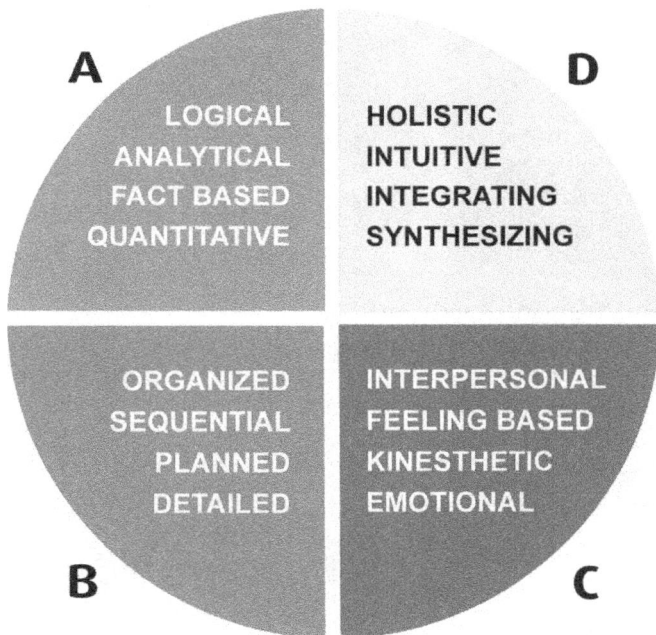

A

LOGICAL
ANALYTICAL
FACT BASED
QUANTITATIVE

D

HOLISTIC
INTUITIVE
INTEGRATING
SYNTHESIZING

ORGANIZED
SEQUENTIAL
PLANNED
DETAILED

INTERPERSONAL
FEELING BASED
KINESTHETIC
EMOTIONAL

B

C

Upper left A **Learners respond to:** Formal lecture Data based content Financial/Technical case discussion Textbooks & bibliographies Program learning	**Upper Right D** **Learners respond to:** Experiential opportunities Free flow Individuality Future oriented discussions Spontaneity Playfulness Visual displays Aesthetics
Lower left B **Learners respond to:** Thorough planning Administrative/organizational Case studies Structure Lectures Sequential order	**Lower right C** **Learners respond to:** Being involved Sensory movement Music People oriented case discussions Group interaction

Introduction to the 4MAT model

Created by Dr. Bernice McCarthy, 4MAT is a process for delivering instruction in a way that appeals to all types of learners and engages, informs, allows for practice and creative use of material learned within each lesson. Although developed as an instructional design tool, 4MAT has evolved into a useful and effective model for communicating clearly. 4MAT methodology uses right/left brain research to create efficient transfer of information and better understanding.

The 4MAT also makes us aware not only of the strengths of right or left-brain processing, but how to take advantage of this knowledge.

The 4MAT model identifies four communication preferences:

Purpose

Information

Application

Possibilities

Through research and feedback, the creator of the 4MAT has organized these preferences in a sequence that, when used, creates communications that are more widely understood.

Individuals are unique; they have preferences for receiving and processing information (left or right brain). People have discovered what works well for them and they lead with these information preferences.

- Some prefer to explore the meaning of things – purpose and causation (They question **WHY**)
- Some look for the concepts – components and information (They question **WHAT**)
- Some look for the operations – utilization and application (They question **HOW**)
- Some prefer to review – variations and possibilities (They question **WHAT IF**)

All learning includes four critical steps:

1. **Engage** – The gaining of attention
2. **Share** - The initial discovery of new information
3. **Practice** – The application of this new information and the gaining of skill in applying it
4. **Perform** – The adaptation of this new information and skill for real world use.

The 4MAT system is designed to provide every student with a preferred task during every lesson. Current brain research confirms that we travel the four-part learning cycle when we take in and make meaning of new information. Dr. McCarthy calls this learning cycle 4MAT. For learning to happen, learners must travel the complete cycle.

All learning includes the asking and answering of four questions. These questions form the cycle of learning. This four-part cycle applies to learning anything.

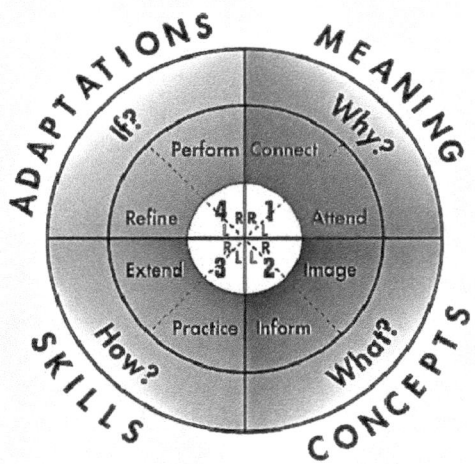

4MAT Lessons
1) Connect
2) Attend
3) Imagine
4) Inform
5) Practice
6) Extend
7) Refine
8) Perform

Although this model appears simple, people respond very positively and with better understanding when communication is structured using the simple order of

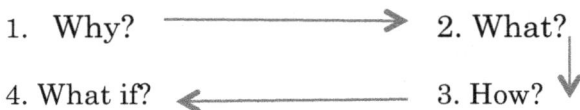

1. Why? ———————⟶ 2. What?

4. What if? ⟵——————— 3. How?

The key to the effectiveness of the 4MAT is to remember that it is a cycle.

You start with the why and then cycle through the what, how and what if.

For example, if you jump around the 4MAT, you may unintentionally "shut down" an individual. Research has shown that individuals who process meanings (whys) will not process anything else until the meaning is established. They won't pay attention to what or how until their "why" is addressed.

People who need the "what" and "how" information will process the "why" first, but eventually their "what" or "how" must be explained.

Selected brain principles

Learning is mental – it comes from the brain.
The learner's brain is unique, specialized and situational.
Individuals have different learning styles.
The brain responds to novelty.
The brain responds to movement.
The brain is always trying to make meaning.
The brain thrives on concrete experiences.
The search for meaning occurs through patterning.
Emotions are critical to patterning.
Emotion is the fast lane to the brain.
People don't pay attention to boring things.
The brain is social.
The brain needs social and environmental interaction.
The brain needs incubation time for memories to form.
The brain needs choice and control of experiences.
Every brain is wired differently.
The brain is changed by experience.
The brain is highly plastic.
The brain connects new information to old.
Exercise boosts brainpower.
Repeat to remember. Short term.
Remember to repeat. Long term.
Stressed brains do not learn the same way as non-stressed brains.
Stimulate more of the senses at the same time.

Vision trumps all over senses. We are powerful and natural explorers.
All learning engages the physiology, the senses. Learning is both conscious and unconscious.

Knowledge is gained through insight, not necessarily transmission and passive knowledge transfer. We need to build more time for self-reflection and conversation in our training.

The brain's day job is not learning, adds neuroscientist John Medina. Medina posits, "The brain is interested in surviving [...] Learning exists only to serve the requirements of this primal goal [...] We do not survive so that we can learn. We learn so that we can survive. [...] If you want a well-educated child, you must create an environment of safety." It is therefore easier for the brain to form new connections when we are in a good mood.

What Medina asserts is equally valid for adult learners. People have to feel safe for their learning to be optimized. In designing training experiences, we need to consider more than just the different ways in which adults learn. We also need to consider ways to increase insight and rewards, and decrease threats. Our brain embraces training that is rewarding and rejects training that feels threatening. Threats, perceived or real, decrease our cognitive performance.

Executive coach and neuro-leadership guru David Rock teaches that there are five important social triggers at play in our brains during every interaction.

Status
Certainty
Autonomy
Relatedness
Fairness

When any of those are invalidated/infirmed, our brains perceive a threat and the pain centers in the brain are activated. When those triggers are validated/affirmed, our brains experience a reward, a surge of dopamine, and the pleasure centers in the brain are activated.

To promote optimal learning, it is crucial that teachers respect every student's sense of status, build awareness of that status, use specific and genuine praise and minimize threats of status differential in the way they speak and relate. It is crucial that teachers provide clear expectations, and break down training into chunks and/or steps to boost students' sense of certainty and control. It is crucial that teachers provide clarity of purpose, and increased control over events to boost students' sense of autonomy. It is crucial that teachers increase trust, connection and empathy. Relatedness is imperative for collaboration. It is also crucial that teachers increase transparency and honesty to boost a sense of fairness in students.

As Bob Lucas stated in <u>Engage your Brain for Learning</u>, "Brain-based learning takes a very learner-centric approach to training." It has been proven to optimize student performance.

1. What can you start doing differently to make your training more brain-friendly?

2. What can you stop doing to make your training more brain-friendly?

3. What are some practical actions you can take to minimize threats and maximize rewards?

Chapter 4

INTENSITY OF ENGAGEMENT

When we maximize student engagement in the classroom, we also maximize buy-in and retention, and enhance the likelihood of learning transfer to the job. When a student is engaged, she experiences a state of flow, a feeling that he or she is 'in the zone.' In this centered state he or she becomes attentive, alert, efficient, and creative; craves information, stimulation, and growth. Maximizing student engagement means keeping students fully present, stimulated, focused and active, physically and mentally energized, and emotionally connected to the learning goals.

Students do better when they work on meaningful activities that necessitate interactions with others. Students expect sensory stimulation. Teachers focusing on students are more attuned to their attention span and will intervene when that attention wanes. Energized and expressive teaching fosters energized and intense learning. Monotony sabotages attention and commitment. Through personal presence, warmth, authenticity, openness and conviction tempered by hints of vulnerability, all backed by thorough preparation and careful pacing, a teacher can win over students.

Teachers are responsible for leading the student-centered classroom. They are in charge of the process of relinquishing more and more of their power to the students. Rather than do more for students, they are responsible for having students say more, give more of themselves and do more for themselves. This requirement needs to be reflected in the very design of the lesson. The outcome of this experience will stay longer with the learners.

What do we mean when we describe something as intense? What do we usually mean when we claim to have an intensive program of instruction? Aren't we basically saying that we spend a lot of time instructing throughout the year? Intensity should have more to do with engagement and the manner of the engagement than with the time spent instructing.

Managing energy, not time, is the key to full engagement. We should seek more learning in less time. Teaching with intensity is about the full engagement of all students at every moment in a class. It is as much about behavior (the teacher's, and the students') as it is about the energy that is leveraged to enhance proficiency in the subject being studied.

Although teachers do not control all the factors that lead students to higher levels of performance, they control the instructional factors, the lesson objectives, the intensity of the activity, and the design of the instruction. Teachers can create high intensity and full engagement activities that both mobilize students' attention and wear them out. The teacher is always responsible for the student-centered learning environment, and in the end accountable for the learning outcomes.

Textbooks and PowerPoint slides don't drive instruction, teachers do! The easiest thing a teacher can do is set an energetic pace at the beginning of every segment of instruction and reset the pace whenever there is a lull. Teacher's and students' energy need to be kept high whenever there is activity in the class.

Real true-to-life events generate high levels of interest in students, so authentic materials should systematically be introduced in support of learning. Authentic materials go a long way in bolstering students' confidence and interest. There are at least three layers of learning embedded within authentic materials: language learning, cultural insights, and practical application.

An older, now retired, colleague of mine shared the following story: "I had been helping a middle-aged, serious professional improve his ability to learn a foreign language for at least a month, five hours a day, and five days a week. Outside the formal classroom, the student was expected to spend another three hours studying on his own with a workbook, a computer, and several CD-ROMs. For class, I had picked what I thought was an excellent textbook, full of drawings and simple, easy to understand explanations. Unfortunately, I utterly failed to connect with that student. He was not learning very fast like others in the class. Most of the time, he seemed bored and impatient with the material. Was it due to a lack of motivation? I wondered. If a student is not paying attention, he is not going to change and improve, I reckoned. Then, one day, I brought a newspaper article written in the target language, and everything changed. The student grew eager to decipher and understand a story that he could glean was about his country, the United States. He worked diligently with a dictionary and grammar book, asked numerous questions, so much so that I felt no longer in control of the situation. Then finally he launched into a tentative and labored, yet intense conversation of the article. I was elated. This experience provided the opening I had sought. I was eventually able to regain influence over the direction of the learning by rewarding, with more stimulating material, the change that had occurred within the student."

This anecdote emphasizes the point that "*Better attention always equals better learning.*" Medina (2008).

Shouldn't a teacher's ultimate goal be to help learners develop a greater degree of independence? What good is it to have students depend on teachers for every aspect of their learning journey? How can they then become lifelong learners? It matters more to teach students how to learn and guide them as they do it. Teachers do well to engage students in a reflection that empowers them to go further, yet again and again.

I had grown frustrated with a memorable fellow because of his continual poor performance and lackadaisical attitude in class. Out of desperation and considering that I would have to flunk him, I gave him a week to prepare to teach the next segment of instruction. I told him he would receive a grade for how well he handled the challenge. When the day came, because I believed him to be lazy, I expected little of him. I nonchalantly called him to the front of the class, ready to take over in case he reneged. To my great surprise, he launched into the lesson with aplomb, showed mastery, and involved everybody. He brought a wide smile to my face. Teaching is the highest form of learning, and he had learned his lesson well.

Professor Benjamin Rifkin provided apt illustrations of intensity of engagement through a series of seven scenarios. Each pair of scenarios below illustrates the importance of designing and implementing learning tasks characterized by high intensity of engagement. At all times in the learning process, all students are fully engaged in active learning in order to make the best use of the limited time they have.

Scenario 1: Speaking and Listening

Low intensity of engagement	High Intensity of Engagement
Entire class listens as students, one at a time, make presentations on the topic of housing (homelessness, gentrification, etc.) in the target culture. While one student speaks, others should be listening, but are daydreaming.	Students listen in pre-assigned groups as members of another group present, in turn, on the same topic. Groups brainstorm questions for the presenter and later debate in groups or teams on the same topic

Scenario 2: Grammar and Lexicon

Low intensity of engagement	High Intensity of Engagement
Students work in groups to fill out a grammar worksheet. When a quicker group finishes, group members sit silently and wait or talk in English about a party on campus this coming weekend.	Students work in groups to fill out a grammar worksheet. When a quicker group finishes, the teacher gives the members of this group two different texts from the internet on the same topic with the challenge of analyzing differences in perspective in the two texts. The texts feature the targeted grammar or lexicon.

Scenario 3: Reading and Speaking

Low intensity of engagement	High Intensity of Engagement
Class "discusses" symbolism in a short story. Students may or may not have read the assigned story, but are reluctant to participate in the discussion. Teacher winds up lecturing in order to "cover the important points" of the day.	Students of each group read a different story on the same topic. In class, students work in groups (by story) to retell the story they read, describe characters. Then they mix up in heterogeneous groups (by story), discussing differences in authorial treatment in each of the different stories they read. Teacher follows up with class discussion on student group conclusions.

Scenario 4: Speaking and Listening

Low Intensity of Engagement	High Intensity of Engagement
All-class discussion of hobbies and interests. Three students dominate the discussion; the rest of the students are silent. When students do speak in discussion, they address (look at) the teacher, ignoring their peers.	Students work in groups to create a survey about hobbies and interests. Teacher checks the surveys for linguistic accuracy. In the next class, students mingle and survey one another, then meet in groups to consolidate data and draw conclusions. Next groups prepare and make presentations, considering both the data and the possibility of survey bias. Teacher follows up with discussion and suggests that students use their surveys to interview native speakers of the target language in the community. (With presentations and conclusions to follow that survey.)

Scenario 5: Culture and Listening
(and reading, writing and speaking)

Low Intensity of Engagement	High Intensity of Engagement
Students listen to teacher's presentation on geography of the target culture. After the presentation, students answer questions. Teacher asks one student at a time, addressing questions to the entire class. Many students do not pay attention to presentation or questions and answers (unless called upon themselves.)	Teacher gives students questions and list of target-culture search engines or websites with geography information. Students read (addition of reading, to this scenario!) printouts of images, and work in groups to create student reports. While one group presents its reports (addition of speaking!), other students are charged with creating questions to ask the presenting group. (Each student must come with three questions for each presentation; each student asks one question in discussion, but turns in, in writing, all three questions to the teacher after the discussion is over, together with notes on any questions answered by the presenting group.)

Scenario 6: Reading and Speaking

Low Intensity of Engagement	High Intensity of Engagement
Students read a short story and come to class prepared to discuss it. Teacher asks a few closed-questions, gets one-word answers or "I don't know" and then lectures for 45 minutes. Students doodle.	Students read the same text and come to class assigned to retell the story from the point of view of another character in the story or of another character from another story. Students may immediately disclose the identity of their chosen perspective or this may be a guessing game for conversation partners as students retell the story to one another. Teachers ask groups to consider how the story would have been different had it been narrated by an American character or had one or more of the characters been American. This leads to a discussion of the national qualities of the text the students have read: "What makes this story Russian [Indonesian? Kenyan? Brazilian?] ?

Scenario 7: Writing

Low Intensity of Engagement	High Intensity of Engagement
Product focused individualized writing assignment: each student writes to the audience of one (teacher).	Multi-phase process-focused collaborative writing assignment with public presentation (publication) and discussion

Managing and increasing the energy level in a classroom through the use of well thought-out, intense, relevant, and meaningful activities is a significant achievement by itself. To increase the likelihood that a training event will achieve its goal, it is equally important to give the event an overall structure. Gagné's nine events of instruction provide a perfect framework for any lesson. Fostering a sense of urgency right from the start; leveraging the power of icebreakers to set the mood, and integrating curiosity gaps to conjure students' natural and powerful need to know, can all contribute to a high intensity, engaging and impactful event.

Fostering a sense of urgency

Early in my career, desperate to find fast and effective ways to bring distracted groups of students to order, I took to observing more senior instructors who had mastered the art of rapidly focusing the attention of their students. The technique that resonated with me the most consisted in writing in big letters, in a far corner of the board, the articulation of the day's lesson. A checkbox was added to precede each item in the articulation. At the beginning of each class, after switching the lights off and on, then standing next to the checkered items, the senior instructor announced, *"There is a lot of material to be covered, as you can see. So, let us get to work."* As the class proceeded, she would then check off each item after it had been covered. Students had a real sense of where they were going and how much was left to cover.

Icebreakers

The term "icebreaker" comes from the expression "break the ice." There are indeed special ships called "icebreakers" that are designed to break up ice in the arctic regions. And just as these ships make it easier for other ships to travel, an icebreaker helps to clear the way for learning to occur by making the learners more comfortable with new and different people in the room.

Icebreakers have gotten a bad rap -- *"all fluff,"* *"not worth the time."* A very "real" reason many object to using icebreakers is a personal preference for task accomplishment over relationship building. However, Ice Breakers can be an effective way of starting a training session as well as a team-building event. They help people get to know each other and buy into the purpose of the event. Here are some of the benefits of using them:

- They help create a positive group atmosphere
- They help people relax
- They help break down social barriers
- They help energize and motivate
- They help people "think outside the box"
- They help people get to know one another

Training when it is done in groups is subject to group dynamics. Icebreakers allow people to take stock, assess the lay of the land, get their head right and settle in. Icebreakers are tools of inclusion. An atmosphere which is conducive to student learning is one in which all students feel included, valued, and respected.

If an icebreaker session is well designed and well facilitated, it can really help get things off to a great start. By getting to know each other and getting to know the trainers, people can become more engaged in the process and can then more willingly contribute to a successful outcome.

When designing our icebreaker, we must think about the "ice" that needs to be broken.

The "ice" may simply be the fact that people have not yet met, and have nagging questions about each other; and/or the status differential; or people's perceptions of each other across lines of difference. We use an icebreaker when participants do not share a similar background, when they need to bond quickly, when the team is newly formed, when the topics under discussion are new or unfamiliar, and when as trainers we need to get to know and have them know us early in the training. Focusing squarely on what is important to the learning event – working towards a common goal, a shared interest in a successful outcome, renders differences moot.

Curiosity Gaps, Mindjogs and Other Hooks

Pique the curiosity of students early. Use curiosity as a primary motivator at the beginning of a lesson by starting with a thought-provoking question or surprising statement. Make students feel that there is a gap in their knowledge. Wake up their curiosity. Make them want to know. The awareness that we do not know something that matters to us creates discomfort. We can also use pre-assessment instruments to create the gap. Load the assessment instrument with meaningful, but little-known facts, or difficult to define concepts. At the beginning of a class on 'Assessing Learning' we used to ask students to define concepts such as ipsative assessment, metacognition, direct measure of assessment. Taken aback, very few could readily answer.

The point was made. They needed the class. Rather than fill the gaps by telling students the answers or the facts, having students realize the gap, and asking them what difference it would make if they knew the missing information, we had their attention. We then either gave them the answers or made them work to find them out.

Gagné's Nine Events of Instruction

In his 1965 book, "The Conditions of Learning", Educational Psychologist, Robert Gagné described a nine-step process called the events of instruction; nine specific steps trainers should follow when supporting and promoting student learning. Gagné and his followers were known as behaviorists, and their focus was on the outcomes - or behaviors - that result from training. The nine events represent a general framework to help make sure the conditions for good instruction and learning are met. While it may not be necessary to cover each of the steps, especially when you have limited time, they provide a guideline for what a good lesson might look like.

The terms, briefing and training, are often used interchangeably. While briefing and training sometimes overlap, the purpose of each is different. The purpose of a briefing is to convey information without any systematic and objective way of verifying across the board, and individually, if and how the information was understood and received. While there may be an opportunity for questions and answers, the briefer's responsibility ends once the information is imparted. Briefing and training activities show up in the Nine Events of Instruction. The first four events apply to both teaching and briefing, and the last five only to training.

The figure below shows these instructional events in the left column and the associated mental processes in the right column:

Instructional Event	Internal Mental Process
1. Gain attention	A stimulus activates receptors
2. Inform learners of objectives	Creates expectations for learning
3. Stimulate recall of prior learning	Retrieval and activation of short-term memory
4. Present the content	Selective perception of content
5. Provide "learning guidance"	Semantic encoding for storage in long-term memory
6. Elicit performance (practice)	Responds to questions to enhance encoding and verification
7. Provide feedback	Reinforcement and assessment of correct performance
8. Assess performance	Retrieval and reinforcement of content
9. Enhance retention and transfer to the job	Retrieval and generalization of learned skill to new situation

Source: Kevin Kruse:
http://www.elearningguru.com/articles/art3_3.htm

Gain attention. Present a problem or a new situation. Start each lesson with a thought-provoking question or interesting fact. Use an "interest device" that grabs the learner's attention. This can be thought of as a *teaser*. The idea is to grab the learners' attention so that they will watch and listen, while you present the learning point. You can use devices such as:

Storytelling

Demonstrations

Presenting a problem to be solved

Doing something the wrong way (the instruction would then show how to do it the right way)

Inform learner of objective. This allows the learners to organize their thoughts around what they are about to see, hear, and/or do. Tell them what they will be able to do by the end of the training event.

Stimulate recall of prior knowledge. This allows the learners to build on their previous knowledge or skills. It is much easier to build on what we already know. Our perceptions are influenced by what we know, what we expect, and what we want to achieve. New information is synthesized from that which is already known.

Present the material. Chunk the information to avoid memory overload. Bloom's Taxonomy and Learning Strategies can be used to help sequence the lesson by helping you chunk them into levels of difficulty. Our brains like to organize perceptions into meaningful units and patterns. We pay attention to information that is meaningful and disregard what is not meaningful to us.

Provide guidance for learning. This is not the presentation of content, rather, instructions on how to learn. This is normally simpler and easier than the subject matter or content. The rate of learning increases; learners are less likely to waste time or become frustrated by basing performance on incorrect facts or poorly understood concepts.

Elicit performance. Practice by letting the learner do something with the newly acquired behavior, skills, or knowledge

Provide feedback. Show correctness of the learner's response. Analyze the learner's behavior. The feedback needs to be specific, not just, "you are doing a good job" Tell them "why" they are doing a good job and elicit and/or provide specific guidance.

Assess performance. Assess to determine if the lesson has been learned.

Enhance retention and transfer. Inform the learner or inquire about similar realistic problem situations, provide additional practice, put the learner in a transfer situation, review the lesson.

The instructional activities listed above can be regarded as a convenient checklist to help trainers design instructional units that are likely to be effective.

Additionally, before learners even go to training, their manager would do well to discuss the need for training and what is expected upon their return. In the conversation, the learners should identify what they need to learn and need to be able to do as a result of the training.

At the beginning of class, there is a benefit to all when learners articulate their expectations of the class, and share what they already know about the subject. Learners should produce some of the material. Learners and trainers should provide questions to frame the discussion and challenge each other's thinking. Learners should be stimulated to produce some of their own learning.

Teaching is like a contact sport. Speaking figuratively, there is a big ball in the hands of a teacher. The ball represents the content of the lesson. In that ball we place lots of powerful questions, key answers, and a lot of passion. Then, we set the ball on fire. Fairly quickly, it must exchange hands, bounce from one person to the next and on and on, and never touch the ground. In a good class everybody has a chance to play with the ball before returning it to its dedicated custodian. Everybody has been touched by the ball never to be the same.

1. What can you do specifically to provide your students with a more intense learning experience?

2. How else can you make the presentation of your material exciting to students?

3. What else could be done to make student learning through engagement more memorable?

Chapter 5

A TEACHER'S WAY OF BEING

A teacher is a vessel, a vessel much like a fancy modern day automobile with GPS, blind spot rear view mirrors, rear camera, and all the things that make you forget it is just a car; yes, a vessel, never an end in itself. Eventually the vessel must fade in the background, stop being the focal point and give prominence to the destination. In a classroom, the new skill, the new knowledge, the new perspective, the new attitude, the new behavior is always the destination. The destination is the prize.

A car invites a ride. On ground, it can take a traveler almost anywhere he or she wants to go. The car has that potential. Whether the traveler appreciates the possibilities is entirely up to him or her. He or she could push the gas or sputter along. Yet, the potential remains there to be tapped into. The car's real power is unrelated to the drivers' skills and desires. So is it with teacher and student. Potential is the means to the end. What matters is getting to the destination.

Yet, even a vessel needs attention once in a while. As a vessel the teacher needs to be in mental, emotional and physical shape to facilitate the trip and deliver her charges to the destination. You must be prepared, motivated, and built in ways that enable you to withstand the journey. Vessels get beaten up. Teachers need be resilient.

You must know who you are, what you are looking for, what you want, what your focus is, what your purpose is, and how to stand in your power. In the end, your job is not to teach, it is to inspire learning and help others think effectively. You would do well to start seeing yourself both as a leader and a process manager. You are an influencer.

Certainly, you must connect with those you lead, establish rapport, a shared purpose for the engagement, you must also convey respect, stop talking and start listening to what the students expect to gain, why they are there with you, what preconceptions and apprehensions they bring to the experience, what they need from you, and what they believe to be true a priori. To be more impactful, teachers must learn to listen to students for understanding, and give students a reason to care and listen to them. How you connect goes a long way in helping you establish working trust, and helping you create an atmosphere conducive to self-disclosure (which you need to assess whether learning is taking place).

To enjoy any measure of credibility and be effective a teacher needs to know what she's talking about cold, which is different from being perfect. A teacher needs to know the content well, become a subject matter expert. A teacher needs to try and slow things down and let students mull over what they have shared with them through an activity (group or individual) or practice of some sort. A teacher needs to give up a lot of the control over the content to the students, and let them share responsibility for the learning. The more control is given to the learners, the more learning occurs. A teacher needs to allow questions to emerge no matter how unexpected they may be. Students need that crucial process to transform information into new knowledge. If you respect the process it is likely new insights will follow. To keep conversations focused, a teacher will benefit from having students use the following or a similar framework for classroom collaboration.

Accountable talk Guidelines:

Stay on topic
Use information that is accurate and appropriate for the topic.
Think deeply about what your partner has to say.

Please place a check mark to indicate what took place.

INDICATORS	NO	YES
Partner(s) pressed for clarification and explanations – *Could you describe what you mean?*		
Partner(s) required justifications of proposals and challenges – *where did you find that information?*		
Partner(s) recognized and challenged misconceptions – *I don't agree because...*		
Partner(s) demanded evidence for claims and arguments – *Can you give an example...*		
Partner(s) interpreted and used each other's statements – *David suggested...*		

Provoke further learning through open questions, silence, listening, through stories you promote in others as illustrations to key points made, instigating disagreements and alternative perspectives while conveying a sense of equality and maintaining respect. Let there be a cacophony of thoughts. It is in this chaos that intersections emerge and new thoughts are teased out.

Yet, what truly matters is inside. It is the way you think, see and feel about the people who have entrusted you to be a good steward of their time, minds, and emotional welfare. Do you see them as pure potential, peers in learning, endowed with vast amounts of embodied wisdom? Or do you look for their flaws and do you judge them? How you show up and relate to them reflects what you have made of them in your mind. No amount of pretending can hide that truth. Do you hold them in positive regard no matter the baggage they bring or do you let that baggage preclude what they can become? Learning is about becoming and judging is about neutralizing. In the process of learning the ego fades in the background, yet real learning is ultimately learning about the self.

Who you are as a teacher affects who the students are as learners. Learning is an inside out process that transforms internalized powerlessness into transcendence. Internalized powerlessness is a fancy way to describe fear. Who we are as teachers matters! How we view ourselves, how we view others, how we feel, and how we view the world, all speak to the biases we bring to our own and other people's experience of learning. Our "stuff" shows up in the classroom.

Teachers are agents of transformation. They take a stand for something bigger than themselves. They must find their voice and then cultivate the emergence of a voice in others. Teachers need to have a vision and convictions. Clarity is knowing what one's teaching is designed to accomplish.

To make your message congruent monitor your non-verbal communication and your ability to listen actively. Teacher presence is both an attitude and a set of behaviors that make you a compelling partner in co-learning. Teachers need technical expertise, knowledge of content, likeability and personal integrity to win the trust of students; teachers also benefit from the ability to punish and reward. But the most effective teachers also use their bodies in ways that influence the outcomes they are after.

You are relaxed about exposing your true identity when you exude high self-esteem. Self-confidence and inner calm enhance your teacher presence. So does having an underlying sense of purpose, a driving force, a set of values and principles that frame your decisions and actions. Being aware of and in touch with your own feelings and the feelings and moods of others and not being afraid to show them are crucial. Articulating a strong vision of what you want creates an intent that others can feel, see and hear, and also enhances your presence as a teacher. Exhibiting high energy in turn elicits a positively energetic response in others. Positive energy makes others feel good. High energy, passion and enthusiasm make the experience of learning with you more desirable.

People will easily forgive a lack of perfection in technique when passion and enthusiasm abound. With a strong presence in the classroom you will be listened to, respected, and followed.

The behaviors consistent with strong teacher presence are:

Posture. (Are you leaning backward, fidgeting, cross-legged, reclined, etc. Good posture -- being comfortable and leaning slightly forward);

Focus. Paying attention to what's going on rather than being caught up in your own thoughts; feeling good and showing it.

Eye contact. Direct, but not sustained in a threatening way.

Gestures and body movement. Non-threatening and not distracting to the person speaking.

Physical Space. Being aware of how close or far you are from the person speaking.

Open body language, attentive stance, voice modulation, appropriate dress style, positive attitude, attitude of gratitude, compassion, making others feel comfortable by being comfortable...

Voice tone, pitch, and volume. Each can influence the message being relayed. Voice speed. Being deliberate and not overly slow or fast with your words.

Other related elements of strong teacher presence include the appropriate use of gestures
- wider, from the shoulders, not the wrist
- facial expressions, animated voice;
- the use of metaphors, contrasts, similes, and analogies; stories and anecdotes, reflection of the group's sentiments;
- the setting of high goals; and conveying confidence that they can be achieved.

A teacher's way of being influences whether or not students will open up, take a chance, trust the process, and surrender to the experience. How we are inside and outside influences how others respond to us. There must be alignment between our intentions and the actions that reflect them. It is our responsibility as agents of transformation to be the people others want to be around and learn from. We have control over our way of being. We have some control over the outcome of our effort.

In Greek, the word charisma means "special gift." The modern Oxford English Dictionary definition of Charisma is "Compelling attractiveness or charm that can inspire devotion in others." Charisma is the ability to communicate a clear, visionary and inspirational message that captivates and motivates an audience. Charisma is rooted in values and feelings. It is influence born of the alchemy that Aristotle called logos, ethos and pathos.

Logos: logic, reason, thought, discourse. The rational principle that governs the Universe.

Ethos: Morality, spirit, character. The moral element that determines a character's action, rather than his thoughts or emotion.

Pathos: passion, emotion, suffering. The quality or power that evoke a feeling.

That is, to persuade others, you must use powerful and reasoned rhetoric, establish personal and moral credibility, and then rouse followers' emotions and passions.

It is a myth that charisma is a gift from God to a select few. That myth was perpetuated through the centuries by Greek mythology and owes much to the self-protecting ideas of the ruling classes. Rulers, leaders, and institutions throughout the ages tended to maintain power by convincing everyone (including themselves) that ordinary people had neither the right nor the ability to achieve any sort of greatness.

We can think of charisma as a force of character. It is closely related to assertiveness. It is the art of connecting with people through everyday skills such as presence, power and warmth. Charisma is a set of behaviors.

The particulars of presence, power and warmth:

Elements of presence: Posture, focus, eye contact, body movement, paying attention to what's going on rather than being caught up in our own thoughts, feeling good and showing it...

Elements of warmth: open body language, attentive stance, voice modulation, dress style, positive attitude, attitude of gratitude, compassion, making others feel comfortable by being comfortable...

Elements of power/Strength: self-confidence, relaxed and calm demeanor, great listening skills, slow measured vocal tempo, absence of nervousness in voice and body, smile, succinct to the point speech, words packed with high value, take up space, alignment of verbal message with non-verbal message, cut out excessive head bobbing, comfortable with silence, deliberate uses of silence and pauses...

We must identify what gets in the way of exuding charisma and the factors that limit personal power.

The obstacles to presence, power and warmth are:

Internal discomfort (physical or mental), physical tension, anxiety, dissatisfaction, self-criticism, self-doubt, negativity...

Lack of self-confidence, lack of enthusiasm, low expectations of others, lack of trust, close-mindedness, wanting to be liked, low self-worth, fear of failure, fear of rejection, critical, fear of taking risks, indecisiveness, controlling attitude, need to be perfect, fear of embarrassment, focus on problems... how can we overcome the obstacle to presence, power, and warmth?

With charisma, you will become more influential, persuasive and inspiring. People will become magnetically drawn to you, trust you more, and want to learn from you.

Power posing

Can posed displays of power cause a person to feel more powerful? Do people's mental and physiological systems prepare them to be more powerful?

Amy Cuddy, an American social psychologist known for her research on nonverbal behavior, asserts that humans and other animals express power through open, expansive postures, and express powerlessness through closed, contractive postures.

But can these postures actually cause power?

High-power posers experience elevations in testosterone, decreases in cortisol, and increased feelings of power and tolerance for risk. Low-power posers, on the other hand, exhibited the opposite pattern. In short, posing in displays of power cause advantageous and adaptive psychological, physiological, and behavioral changes, and these findings suggest that embodiment extends beyond mere thinking and feeling, to physiology and subsequent behavioral choices.

That a person can, by assuming two simple 1-min poses, embody power and instantly become more powerful has very important real-world, actionable implications.

High power posers performed better and were more likely to be chosen for hire. In both human and non-human primates, expansive, open postures reflect high power, whereas contractive, closed postures reflect low power. Not only do these postures reflect power, they also *produce* it; in contrast to adopting low power poses, adopting high power poses increases explicit and implicit feelings of power and dominance, risk-taking behavior, action orientation, pain tolerance, and testosterone (the dominance hormone), while reducing stress, anxiety, and cortisol (the stress hormone).

Moreover, adopting high-power poses leads to stronger effects on thought abstraction and action. The acquisition of power causes individuals to feel more positive, in control, and optimistic about the future, and to become more goal-oriented and likely to take action. Given that it is often difficult or risky to overtly change the power dynamics in such a situation, assuming a high-power pose represents a subtle way of making oneself feel more powerful.

Furthermore, high testosterone and low cortisol, a hormone profile that is characteristic of high-status and effective leaders and is induced by power posing, is associated with reduced stress, increased sense of personal control, and increased engagement and performance in competitive tasks. The high-power posers, in contrast to low-power posers, appeared to better maintain their composure, project more confidence, and present more captivating and enthusiastic speeches, in turn leading to higher overall performance evaluations.

Charisma is largely in the eyes of the beholders. It is a fantasy. However, it is important to decide what you are going to do with that fantasy, whether you are going to use it to accelerate learning or for more sinister ends.

When we become more responsive in our teaching, others become more responsive in listening and learning.

The four principles of Responsive Teaching:
From Arbinger - The Choice in Teaching and Education

Principle 1: "I am not the Teacher"

My job is not to teach. It is to inspire learning. Four principles of responsive teaching help me to inspire learning in all that I do.

They keep me seeing people as people. They keep me living and teaching the responsive way. They invite responsiveness and learning in those I would teach. These principles are the pillars upon which the most successful and inspiring teaching is built.

I am not the teacher. There is a teacher; it just isn't the teacher. The curious soul that resides deep inside everyone is the real teacher.

What does the first principle — I am not the teacher — mean in actual practice?

It means that I must avoid the temptation of teachers – the inclination to see the people in front of me as my students.

Yes, they are students, but that does not mean they are mine. I guide, instruct, facilitate, and help, but that does not make me the teacher. The teacher is the one who seals learning in heart and mind, and I am not that person.

I do not place thoughts on the shelves of others' minds, nor can I instill conviction. My words however brilliant, do not teach, but mingle – with the words and thoughts of those who listen.

The conversation within is where learning happens, and therefore teaching as well. Metacognition matters.

What do I do when I feel smarter, cleverer, or more insightful?

I talk more and ask less. I think of myself more and others less. I worry about my reputation more and other's learning less.

"The person who 'loves' teaching or 'hates' teaching is too concerned about himself to inspire learning." Arbinger

Principle 2: "My Obligation is to Learn"

So how can I as an educator, point the way to the teacher within my students?

There is only one-way: by being a lively student of that teacher myself.

Students learn best by watching others learn, not by watching others teach.

The master teacher is nothing more than a master learner who has remembered the art of childhood—the art of learning in the presence of others; or more precisely the art of learning because of the presence of others. There can be no learning without conversation with a person (or their thoughts or idea) and therefore no teaching as well.

The master teacher creates a conversation for students to enter —a dialogue with great minds and their ideas – and then invites the students to join him by valuing their ponderings above his own.

A master teacher teaches, yes. But he is effective because he remembers to learn.

Whether I, or others know a lot or a little, what I communicate is my passion, or lack of passion, for learning.

If learning is my obligation, what is it that I must learn? To begin with, everything that I can about those that I am to teach; their names, their interests, their struggles, their talents and abilities. Above all else I must learn to care about those I have been charged to teach. If I don't care, neither will they.

To one who would teach, the eye, mouth and ear have a single purpose: they are organs of listening and learning. Every moment in front of a class is a moment of learning – or should be. If I listen, I will feel the energy or lack of energy in the room, see the interest or lack of interest in students' eyes, hear the agreement or discomfort in people's voices.

The act of teaching requires the art of moment-to-moment learning.

Principle 3: "I See Greatness"

In my teaching, I must always remember that each student has the capacity to be my mentor.

I am most successful as a teacher when I see those I teach as mentors already.

I must teach to the potential greatness in them. For those I teach become as I see them. The gifted student responds to my challenges and faith. The challenging student responds to my frustration and fear. The slower student slows to the pace I expect. Some of the greatness in my students is obvious. Much, however, is not. I must look for it. But to look is to find, for greatness is in all. Learning, sociability and ability, all are increased by teachers who focus on the best in their students.

My task as one who would teach is to look for greatness within others. Greatness lives in each of us, but only in proportion to the degree we don't concern ourselves with it. Or put another way, only in proportion to the degree we focus on the greatness that is in others. Brilliance that is blind to its own brilliance inspires; genius that glories in the genius of others, uplifts. He who is taken by his own cleverness makes one both wary and weary.

The person who is truly learning and growing inside is truly curious and full of questions without. I must live, instruct, assign, and discuss in ways that honor and invite curiosity. We learn most when expectations and demands are highest. It is easier to expect less, for less demands less of us. At least this is what resistance thinks.

Principle 4: "I Build Community"

Responsiveness invites cooperation, consideration, and openness. Learning happens in relationship with others. The quality and quantity of learning is a function of the quality of the relationships in which the learning takes place. When people learn together, they feel uplifted, fulfilled, excited, inspired. This is education at its best – education as it should be. Education as it is among the master teachers in our neighborhoods, children at play.

Those who were responsive to me awakened responsiveness within. I opened my heart and mind to what we were learning. Behind every topic I now love there is a teacher who once loved me. My interest is a reflection of theirs.

The influence I have regarding what I would teach depends on the feeling of community in our learning. Make the deep change from resistance to responsiveness, and everything in life gets better. Way of being is the most important factor of all. Way of being determines influence. The effectiveness of any educational effort ultimately depends on the educator's personal way of being.

1. How do you show up in the classroom?

2. How do you stand in your power?

3. How do you use your body to increase your influence?

4. What gets in the way of you showing up powerfully?

5. What limits your personal power?

Chapter 6

TEACHING IN THE INTERROGATIVE

"Asking a question is the simplest way of focusing thinking ... asking the right question may be the most important part of thinking."
Edward de Bono

Thinking is a question and answer process. Most people presume that our thoughts are only statements. Our thoughts take the form of both statements and questions. Thinking is not driven by answers but by questions. Questions define tasks, express problems, and delineate issues. Answers on the other hand, often signal a full stop in thought. Once we think we have an answer we stop thinking. Only when an answer generates another question does thought continue. Students need questions to turn on their intellectual engines and they need to generate questions from teachers' questions to get their thinking to go somewhere. If we want thinking we must stimulate it with questions that lead students to further questions. Superficial questions betray superficial understanding.

"Students who have good questions are really thinking and learning." (Linda Elder: 1999)

Questions are fundamental for learning, for gathering information, for building and maintaining relationships, for thinking clearly, creatively, and critically, for making requests, and for initiating action. Asking questions is fundamental for resolving conflicts and breakdowns, making decisions, solving problems, instigating out of the box thinking, innovating, listening fully, and managing change. Questions open our minds and shake our view of the world. New questions can totally shift our perspectives, moving us into fresh ways of looking at and solving problems. Questions drive results. The results you get will be driven by the questions you ask. Sub-par questions produce sub-par results. Questions are the engines of profound transformations.

Powerful questions are open-ended, and are not looking for a specific answer. They promote thought. Powerful questions are positive. Their focus remains on improvement and continuous learning. Not only does the quality of an answer depend on the quality of the question, it is not even possible to get the best answers without the best questions. Breakthroughs in thinking depend on provocative questions. Great questions empower people, and instill in them a sense of their own efficacy. The most effective questions create clarity, help people think, inspire people to look at things differently, and challenge assumptions. The most powerful questions start with: *How* or *What*, not *Why*, *When*, *Who* or *Does*... that is not to say that other questions are not important. They have a place and a role to play, but hardly produce as much insight as *How* and *What* questions are capable of producing.

Effective questioning skills are among the most valuable skills that a teacher can possess. If you ask the wrong questions, you'll probably get the wrong answers, or at least not quite what you're hoping for. Asking the right question is at the heart of effective communication and information exchange. By using the right questions in a particular situation, you can improve a whole range of communication skills: for example, you can gather better information and learn more; you can build stronger relationships, manage people more effectively, and help others learn too. You can avoid misunderstanding, diffuse a heated situation, and persuade people. Questions are great for keeping people engaged. Questions are useful to identify gaps in knowledge and initiate disequilibrium that results in a changed knowledge structure.

To be effective, questions must be purposeful. You must be clear as to the kind of thinking that is required to answer the questions you ask. Remembering, applying, analyzing, evaluating, or creating. Questions can be divergent or convergent. Convergent questions have a single correct answer, (questions about concrete facts.) Divergent questions have no single correct answer, and many answers are possible.

Using Questioning Techniques

Here are some common questioning techniques, and when (and when not) to use them:

Open and Closed Questions

A closed question usually receives a single word or a very short, factual answer. For example, "Are you thirsty?" The answer is "Yes" or "No"; "Where do you live?" The answer is generally the name of your town or your address.

Open questions elicit longer answers. They usually begin with interrogative pronouns such as what, why, how. An open question asks the respondent for his or her knowledge, opinion, or feelings. "Tell me" and "describe" can also be used in the same way as open questions. Here are some examples:

What happened at the meeting? Why did he react that way? How was the party? Tell me what happened next. Describe the circumstances in more detail.

Open questions are good for developing an open conversation, (What did you do on vacation?), finding out more detail, (What else do we need to do to make this a success?), finding out the other person's opinion or issues, (What do you think about those changes?)

Closed questions are good for testing your understanding or the other person's, (So, if I get this qualification, I will get a raise?), concluding a discussion or making a decision, (Now we know the facts, are we all agreed this is the right course of action?), frame setting, (Are you happy with the service from your bank?)

A misplaced closed question, on the other hand, can kill the conversation and lead to awkward silences, so these are best avoided when a conversation is in full flow.

Funnel Questions

This technique involves starting with general questions, and then homing in on a point in each answer, and asking more and more detail at each level. Detectives taking a statement from a witness often use it:

"How many people were involved in the fight?"
"*About ten.*"
"Were they kids or adults?"
"*Mostly kids.*"
"What were their ages?"
"*About fourteen or fifteen.*"
"Were any of them wearing anything distinctive?"
"*Yes, several of them had red baseball caps on.*"
"Can you remember if there was a logo on any of the caps?"
"*Now you come to mention it, yes, I remember seeing a big letter B.*"

Using this technique, the investigator has helped the witness re-live the scene and gradually focus on a useful detail. Perhaps he will be able to identify the people wearing a hat like this from video-surveillance footage. It is unlikely he would have gotten this information if he had simply asked an open question such as "Are there any details you can give me about what you saw?"

When you use the funnel questioning technique, start with closed questions. As you progress through the tunnel, start using more open questions.

Funnel questions are good for finding out more detail about a specific point, (What more can you tell me about Option B.), gaining the interest or increasing the confidence of the person you're speaking with, (Have you used the IT Helpdesk? Did they solve your problem? And what was the attitude of the person who took your call?)

Probing Questions

Asking probing questions is another strategy for finding out more detail. Sometimes it is as simple as asking your respondent for an example, to help you understand a statement they have made. At other times, you need additional information for clarification, "When do you need this report by, and do you want to see a draft before I give you my final version?", or to investigate whether there is proof for what has been said, "How do you know that the new database can't be used by the sales force?" An effective way of probing is to use the 5 Ws method (what, when, who, where, why), which can help you quickly get to the root of a problem.

Use questions that include the word "exactly" to probe further: "What exactly do you mean by fast-track?", "Who, exactly, wanted this report?" Probing questions are good for gaining clarification to ensure you have the whole story and that you understand it thoroughly and for drawing information out of people who are trying to avoid telling you something.

Leading Questions

Leading questions try to lead the respondent to your way of thinking. They can do this in several ways:

With an assumption, "How late do you think the project will be delivered?" This assumes that the project will certainly not be completed on time.

By adding a personal appeal to agree at the end: "Lori's very efficient, don't you think?" or "Option B is better, isn't it?"

By phrasing the question so that the "easiest" response is "yes" (our natural tendency to prefer to say "yes" than "no" plays an important part in the phrasing of referendum questions):

"Shall we all approve Option B?" is more likely to get a positive response than "Do you want to approve option B or not?". A good way of doing this is to make it personal. For example, "Would you like me to go ahead with Option B?" rather than "Shall I choose Option B?"

By giving people a choice between two options, both of which you would be happy with, rather than the choice of one option or not doing anything at all. Strictly speaking, the choice of "neither" is still available when you ask "Which would you prefer, A or B", but most people will be caught up in deciding between your two preferences. Leading questions tend to be closed.

Leading questions are good for getting the answer you want but leaving the other person feeling that they have had a choice. They are also good for closing a sale: (If that answers all of your questions, shall we agree on a price?)

Use leading questions with care. If you use them in a self-serving way or one that harms the interests of the other person, then they can, quite rightly, be seen as manipulative and dishonest.

Rhetorical Questions

Rhetorical questions are not really questions at all, in that they do not expect an answer. They are really just statements phrased in question form: "Isn't John's design work so creative?"

People use rhetorical questions because they are engaging for the listener - as they are drawn into agreeing ("Yes it is and I like working with such a creative colleague") - rather than feeling that they are being "told" something like "John is a very creative designer". (To which they may answer "So what?")

Rhetorical questions are even more powerful if you use a string of them. "Isn't that a great display? Don't you love the way the text picks up the colors in the photographs? Doesn't it use space really well? Wouldn't you love to have a display like that for our products?"

Rhetorical questions are good for engaging the listener.

Other strategies to promote student thinking:

Think pair-share

Asking students to unpack their thinking by describing how they arrived at an answer.

Asking summaries of individual responses and class responses to questions.

Using hypothetical thinking: What would happen if...?

Using analogies: How is this like...?

You have probably used all of these questioning techniques before in your everyday life, at work, and at home. By consciously applying the appropriate kind of questioning, you can gain the information, response, or outcome that you want even more effectively.

Response time

Make sure that you give the person you are questioning enough time to respond. This may need to include thinking time before they answer, so do not just interpret a pause as a "No comment," and plow on. Give them at least seven seconds before you say another word, and do not answer your own question. Let silence do the heavy lifting.

Skillful questioning needs to be matched by careful listening so that you understand what people really mean with their answers. Good questions often come from good listening. Your body language and tone of voice can also play a part in the answers you get when you ask questions. How teachers respond to students' answers is also very important. If an answer is correct but hesitant, the teacher should give the student feedback about why the answer is correct. This provides an opportunity to explain the material again. If the student is unsure, others may be confused as well.

If the answer is completely wrong, but a serious attempt was made, you should probe for more information, give clues, simplify the question, review the previous steps, or re-teach the material. If the answer is silly or careless, it is better to correct it and move on.

Students should learn and be encouraged to ask questions effectively to break out of the recitation mode. Recitation occurs when the teacher initiates questions and students respond. More than recitation, we need communication. Communication is the exchange of meaning. It is my attempt to let you know what I mean. Communication includes any behavior that another human being perceives and interprets: it is your understanding of what I mean. Communication includes sending both verbal messages (words) and nonverbal messages (tone of voice, facial expression, behavior, and physical setting). It includes consciously sent messages as well as messages that the sender is totally unaware of sending. Whatever I say and do, even through my pauses and stillness, I communicate. Communication, therefore, involves a complex, multilayered, dynamic process through which we exchange meaning.

Every communication has a message sender and a message receiver. The sent message is never identical to the received message. Why? Communication is indirect; it is a symbolic behavior. Ideas, feelings, and pieces of information cannot be communicated directly but must be externalized or symbolized before being communicated. Encoding describes the producing of a symbol message. Decoding describes the receiving of a message from a symbol. The message sender must encode his or her meaning into a form that the receiver will recognize—that is, into words and behavior. Receivers must then decode the words and behavior—the symbols—back into messages that have meaning for them. The greater the difference in background between senders and receivers, the greater the difference in meanings attached to particular words and behaviors may be.

Communication does not necessarily result in understanding. Miscommunication occurs when the interlocutor does not receive the sender's intended message. Communication continually involves misunderstanding caused by misperception, misinterpretation, and misevaluation. When the sender of a message comes from one culture and the receiver from another, the chances of accurately transmitting a message are more questionable. Perception is the process by which each individual selects, organizes, and evaluates stimuli from the external environment to provide meaningful experiences for himself or herself. Perceptual patterns are selective, learned, culturally determined, consistent, and inaccurate.

Perception is *selective*. At any one time, there are too many stimuli in the environment for us to observe. Therefore, we screen out most of what we see, hear, taste, and feel. We screen out the overload and allow only selected information through our perceptual screen to our conscious mind. Typically, we take in only what supports our view of the world, what makes sense to us. Perceptual patterns are *learned*. We are not born seeing the world in one particular way. Our experience teaches us to perceive the world in certain ways. Perception is *culturally determined*. We learn to see the world in a certain way based on our cultural background. Perception tends to remain *constant*. Once we see something in a particular way, we continue to see it that way. *We therefore see things that do not exist, and do not see things that do exist.* Our interests, values, and culture act as filters and lead us to distort, block, and even create what we choose to see and hear. We perceive what we expect to perceive. We perceive things according to what we have been trained to see.

Interpretation occurs when an individual gives meaning to observations and their relationships; it is the process of making sense out of perceptions. Interpretation organizes our experience to guide our behavior. Based on our experience, we make assumptions about our perceptions so we will not have to rediscover meanings each time we encounter similar situations. Since we are constantly bombarded with more stimuli than we can absorb and more perceptions than we can keep distinct, we only perceive those images that may be meaningful. We group perceived images into familiar categories that help to simplify our environment, become the basis for our interpretations, and allow us to function in an otherwise overly complex world.

Perhaps the most difficult skill in communication involves standing back from yourself, or being aware that you do not know everything, that a situation may not make sense, that your guesses may be wrong, and that the ambiguity in the situation may continue. In this sense, the ancient Roman dictum "knowledge is power" becomes true. In knowing yourself, you gain power over your perceptions and reactions; you can control your own behavior and your emotional reactions to others' behavior. Communication confronts us with limits to our perceptions, our interpretations, and our evaluations and thus provides impetus for discovery.

Is Anyone Listening?

Let's start with the assumptions that better communication is the key to our ability to be more productive together; that better communication requires conversations and that the conversation is the relationship. How would you challenge these assumptions? What are the biggest causes of breakdowns in your relationships?

Choose between the following:

a. My own listening and attitude.
b. Other people's listening and attitude.

More often than not when misunderstandings or conflicts occur, most people think it's someone else's fault. "If only they had listened better. If only they'd communicated more clearly." What if as Chantal Burns claims *"People and relationships don't get stuck? Only thinking gets stuck."* What then would the implications be for you? Our own thinking, not someone else's, generates our responses, behaviors, and actions.

Whenever we have an issue with someone else, that issue is caused by how we think about them and about what they are saying. We could choose to think differently. When we realize we're in the driver's seat, we get to choose when we stop.

It is important to know the answer to the question "why am I talking?" W.A.I.T., and equally important to know the answer to the question "why am I listening? [W.A.I.L.] When we listen to confirm or validate what we already know, we're listening from the past. We're in a reactive mode. Listening in this way acts as an obstacle and stops us from truly hearing something new or different that may advance our thinking. When we listen to understand, we choose to focus outward despite what we already know. We open ourselves to receive. We become curious. We make ourselves fully available and responsive to others. This mode of listening gives us access to everything we need in communication. It allows us to get out of our own way and forge deep connections with others.

Unfortunately, listening is often thought of as a burden we impose on ourselves for the benefit of someone else. It is said, "Listening requires more intelligence than talking does." It is the first step in strengthening teamwork, a powerful strategy to optimize our time, and exponentially increasing our productivity. Listening is the ultimate mark of respect; the heart and soul of engagement; the basis for true collaboration; the engine of superior execution; the key to learning, the sine qua non of creativity and innovation. Listening is profitable, and it increases your influence.

Poor listening is a common affliction. A good listener will have curiosity, that all essential desire to learn. That requires a degree of humility, the key to having an open mind. For if you think you know it all, or at least, if you believe you know more than the person to whom you are talking, you are hardly inclined to listen. Listening is a powerful indicator of how you regard someone ... as a person or as an object.

Most people if they listen at all, listen to respond, not to learn. Have you ever talked to someone who was so present with you that it unnerved you? Someone whose full attention was locked on you? Their focus so completely yours that it made you feel as if you were the only person in the world? Someone who made you feel really seen, and really heard? The skill of listening is essential to transformation. How long will someone follow and hear you if they never feel that their voice is really heard?

What is Facilitation?

When a teacher uses facilitation, she blurs the line between teaching and learning. She, in effect, helps students teach themselves. She provides an experience that makes them more responsible for their learning. She becomes a learning facilitator.

Facilitation is a process of enabling groups to collaborate effectively to get work done. Facilitation consists in leading a process of exploration and discovery, or a learning event from a stance of neutrality, with questions.

Facilitation is about helping groups, stay on task, be more creative, productive, and make better decisions. Facilitation is a way to teach in the interrogative without a predetermined notion of what the outcome will look like.

A facilitator does not give firm opinions or solve problems for participants. A facilitator's role is to create the context in which the solutions appear and are expressed by the participants. A facilitator's role is to create disruption, the essence of change, through great questions that elicit great responses that move the process forward. Probing, framing, redirecting, validating, highlighting areas of divergence and agreements, monitoring, maintaining focus, listening, encouraging participation and reflection, and managing the energy in the room are all very useful skills for a facilitator. On occasions, facilitators must intervene differently and instruct to shape the learning process and reorient the group's work.

No matter what facilitators do, and who they are, they have to show up authentically. They must show empathy and demonstrate acceptance of others. When they fail to show up authentically, the event suffers. They must speak the truth, directly, clearly, and concisely. They must remain present in the here-and-now, speak about what is going on right in the moment for them, and encourage others to do the same.

Participants want to feel that their experiences are respected before they can be expected to show up authentically. Who they are must be enough if we expect them to take a chance and speak up. Facilitation is a way of teaching in the interrogative without a net. Telling people what they should do rests on an authoritarian model of interaction. When you ask students what the next step in their learning is, you give them a chance to set their own goals. It is a far superior strategy to get all the minds working on what needs to change rather than to convince each person to do what we think is best. This method is also more respectful and effective.

The person being questioned is responsible for figuring out what they need to do. Learning facilitators simply listen, ask powerful questions, rephrase, and reflect what they are hearing. They reframe if necessary and help students see their own path forward through the learning. Teachers' opinions ultimately will not be as empowering to students as students' own opinions and emotions. Emotions accompany the processing of new and unsettling information as well as the answering of powerful questions, and can ultimately help students work through their resistance to new ideas, and create forward movement.

Teaching in the interrogative does not mean that lecturing has no place in training. It means that we do less lecturing and more facilitating. When learning matters, why attend training if all it entails is passive listening? What would be the difference between going to training and listening to a podcast? It is what you do in class, your conversation, your activity, and your participation that sets training apart. It is through students' manipulation of the material that learning sticks. As a teacher, you first must inform, then excite, then put on your learning facilitator cap in order to involve and empower. Table 1: Student-centered and Teacher centered continuum:

Teacher-centered Learning	Student-centered Learning
Low level of student choice	High level of student choice
Power is primarily with the teacher	Power is primarily with the student

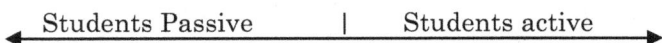

Students Passive	Students active

Source: Geraldine O'Neill and Tim McMahon - University College Dublin

The shift that is required is a shift in the power relationship between the student and the teacher. As a learning facilitator, your role is one of servant-leadership; it is "power with" rather than "power over." (Tree Bressen: Group Facilitation Primer). Teachers' work is to give away their power through more reliance on active rather than passive learning, an emphasis on deep learning and understanding, increased responsibility and accountability on the part of the student, developing an increased sense of autonomy in the learner; encouraging independence in the learner, mutual respect within the learner teacher relationship, and a continuous reflexive approach to the teaching and learning process on the part of both teacher and learner. Good teaching is, oftentimes, just getting out of the students' way and letting them explore.

Facilitation Model
Processing an Activity

Facilitation model adapted from Weaver, Richard G. and Farrell, John D. 1999. Managers as Facilitators.

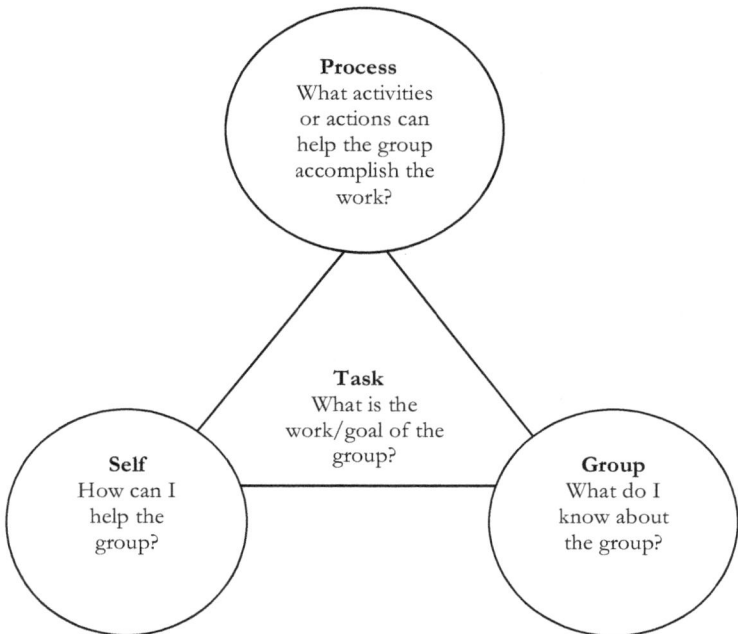

Facilitators help people think. To do that successfully it helps for them to remember and have others emulate, in their sessions, what effective thinkers do:

Effective thinkers:

-Consider a variety of points of view
-Analyze concepts, theories and explanations
-Clarify issues and conclusions
-Raise questions
-Identify assumptions and biases
- Transfer ideas to new content and contexts
-Evaluate beliefs
-Generate novel ideas
-Compare ideas
-Compare ideals with actual practice
-Examine assumptions
-Distinguish relevant information from irrelevant information
-Examine implications
-Come to terms with inconsistencies and contradictions
-Monitor their thoughts and behaviors
-Listen with understanding and empathy

"*Any situation in which some men prevent others from engaging in the process of inquiry is one of violence ... to alienate humans from their own decision making is to change them into objects.*"

Paulo Freire

1. What strategic questions could drive your instruction?

2. Some students fail to appreciate teacher-led questions; they see having to answer questions as doing a teacher's job. What could you say to make them understand the importance of questions?

3. Why do you typically ask questions in class? What is your intent?

4. How else have you been successful in promoting student thinking?

Chapter 7

ASSESSMENT AS LEARNING

The Key to Better Learning

Learning is random and intentional, conscious and unconscious, fragmentary and systematic, disorganized and organized, rational and emotional. People pay attention to and remember what resonates with them, regardless of trainer's intent. The crucial question then becomes how can we ensure that learners actually learn what we intend for them to learn? Classroom assessment is the basis for decisions that teachers make about, among other things, what to focus on and how to deliver content. It is the basis for decisions that students make – about their feelings of self-worth, and their willingness to engage deeper in the work, among other things. Research conducted in New Zealand by Terry Crooks, in 1988, concluded that classroom assessment has both short and long-term effects on learning. In the short-term, classroom assessment can:

Focus attention on important aspects of a subject

Give students opportunities to practice skills and consolidate learning

Guide further learning activities

In 1999, the Assessment Reform Group, in England, indicated that classroom assessment that promotes learning

> ➤ Is embedded as an essential part of teachers' views of teaching and learning
> ➤ Involves sharing learning goals with students
> ➤ Aims to help students to know and to recognize the standards they are aiming for
> ➤ Involve students in self-assessment
> ➤ Provides feedback which leads to students recognizing their next steps and how to take them
> ➤ Is underpinned by confidence that every student can improve
> ➤ Involves both teachers and students reflecting on assessment data.

Improving learning through assessment depends on five, deceptively simple, key factors:

> ➤ The provision of effective feedback to [students];
> ➤ The active involvement of [students] in their own learning;
> ➤ Adjusting teaching to take account of the results of assessment;

➤ A recognition of the profound influence assessment has on the motivation and self-esteem of [*students*], both of which are crucial influences on learning;

➤ The need for [*students*] to be able to assess themselves and understand how to improve.

(Black, P. & William, D. 1999. *Assessment for Learning: Beyond the Black Box,* Assessment Reform Group, University of Cambridge, School of Education)

On one occasion, in an attempt to explain the meaning of the word assessment, I sat down next to a rather large and imposing student. He sat up. My invading his personal space changed the dynamic between us and within him. His posture changed. I was looking at him directly, smiling, and asking probing questions. A dialogue ensued. He disclosed quite a bit about how he was feeling about what he had experienced in the class until then, about what he related to, and what had not worked for him. The point was made. Assessment, which comes from the Latin *assidere* means "to sit down next to" the learner. It is a process that enables one to get a sense for where the learner is in his learning, to take the pulse of the situation, and uncover the processing thoughts that are responsible for the quality of the student's learning. Through assessments students become more aware of not only what they are learning, but also how they are learning it.

Assessment can be understood as systematic information collection to provide feedback without making judgments of worth.

The feedback that follows assessment must contain three elements: recognition of the desired learning goal and objective, evidence about present position, and some understanding of a way to close the gap between the two. Assessment uncovers areas that need attention. Through my dialogue with the rather imposing student, I was able to have him make what was invisible and unclear to the rest of the class visible and clear, uncover what he was saying to himself about what he was learning or not learning, and find out what he was thinking about what he had been exposed to. That process of surfacing a learner's self-talk as he is learning is known as metacognition -- thinking about thinking, or, in our case, thinking about how one is learning. Self-talk truly is the gateway to learning. By coaxing it out, and engaging it, we can help students learn better.

"Self-talk is the internal dialogue one uses to support construction and maintenance of understanding" --Benson, (1993; 2004).

All our actions are driven by internal questions that we may or may not be aware of asking ourselves. Internal questions and answers can produce visible results (reactions, behaviors). Through deliberate attention to metacognition as an essential part of instruction, those internal questions can be brought to light, and the right responses induced to ensure the desired results. You, the teacher, must basically play the metacognition detective to uncover students' thinking. Only then can we confirm that it is on track, or in need of redirection. What students ask themselves and say to themselves internally, is more powerful in determining the next step in the learning than what any teacher may say (unless students have already internalized the teaching points) and is far more likely to determine future behavior.

"In reality, it is through classroom assessment that attitudes, skills, knowledge, and thinking are fostered, nurtured, and accelerated or stifled." --Hynes (1991)

It is only when teachers encourage the outward expression of self-talk that teachers can intervene, begin to address, and fill the gaps in student understanding and knowledge. Teaching without assessment is just talking. In instruction, the goal can never simply be to impart knowledge. Knowledge is only a step. The real goal is understanding. What students know they quickly forget, especially if they truly never understood it. What they understand they can give life to, own, rephrase and explain in their own words. The best way to assess understanding is always through authentic applications, or situations that showcase relevant real-world tasks.

"We use the general term assessment to refer to all those activities undertaken by teachers -- and by their students in assessing themselves -- that provide information to be used as feedback to modify teaching and learning activities. Such assessment becomes formative when the evidence is actually used to adapt the teaching to meet student needs."

Black, P. & William, D. 1998. *Inside the Black Box: Raising standards through classroom assessment*, King's College, London

Do you remember what assessment looked like and felt like in High School?

How did teachers ensure that you learned and understood what they taught you?

What did you like about that? Why? What didn't you like? Why not?

Did assessment in High School look anything like this?

- Teachers' tests encouraged rote and superficial learning.
- There was a tendency to emphasize quantity and presentation of work and to neglect its quality in relation to learning.
- The grading functions were over-emphasized.

- Students were compared with one another. Low attainments were attributed to lack of ability.

"*While assessment has the potential to improve learning for all students, historically it has acted as a barrier rather than a bridge to educational opportunity. Assessments have been used to label students and put them in dead end tracks. Traditional tests have been soundly criticized as biased and unfair to minority students. And, the assessment of language minority students has been particularly problematic.*"

Dietel, R.J., Herman, J.L., Knuth, R.A. 1991. *What Does Research Say About Assessment?* North Central Regional Education Laboratory, Oak Brook.

Purposes of Assessment

In assessment, purpose is everything. Why are we doing it? Assessment for assessment's sake is a waste of everyone's time. Learning is more important than grading, so the type of assessments that we should be promoting puts the focus entirely on learning. Learning is about becoming. It should place the student at the center of the experience and as such require him or her to take greater responsibility. The bottom line about assessment is that we, teachers, should involve learners in the design of their own assessment.

It bears repeating that assessment, "Assidere," means to sit beside. It consists in making student's thinking visible to both teacher and student so that both become more aware of not only what they are learning, but also how they are learning it. Effective assessment is ongoing and continuous. Teachers should be constantly collecting informal and formal information about what and how students are learning, checking student assignments, listening to small-group activities, and observing students engaged in structured and unstructured activities. Teachers can then use the information collected for purposes ranging from communicating with stakeholders to meeting standards and benchmarks.

When teachers systematically collect the right kind of information and use it effectively, they help students grow as thinkers and learners. In some contexts, the terms assessment and evaluation are interchangeable. Here we use the term "assessment" to refer specifically to all kinds of methods and strategies that provide information about student learning with a view towards improving it. Evaluation is the assignment of value – a measurement. Evaluation is the process of making definitive judgments regarding the appropriateness of some person, program, process, or product for a specific purpose.

Summative assessment takes place at the end of a unit or project and gives students and teachers information about the skills and knowledge that students have acquired. It takes place one time and at the end of the learning event. For students it is very akin to an evaluation. Teachers can use them to readjust their instruction the next time around.

On the other hand, formative assessment provides learners with feedback about how they are doing throughout the learning process as it unfolds. Using a broad variety of assessments throughout the instructional cycle can provide valuable information to both the teacher and the learners. Formative assessment can be used to:

- Gauge students' prior knowledge and readiness
- Encourage self-direction and collaboration
- Provide diagnostic feedback to teacher and student
- Monitor progress
- Check for understanding and encourage metacognition
- Demonstrate understanding and skill

Embedded and on-going assessment provides a way for students to show and discover what they know in different ways. With assessment integrated throughout a unit of instruction, teachers learn more about their students' needs and can adjust instruction to improve student achievement. McMillan (2000) explains, "When assessment is integrated with instruction, it informs teachers about what activities and assignments will be most useful, what level of teaching is most appropriate, and how summative assessments provide diagnostic information."

What is the difference between formative and summative assessment?

Activities associated with *summative assessment* (Assessment *of* Learning) result in an evaluation of student achievement, a letter, or grade, which might later appear in a report. Summative assessment is also a necessary aspect of education, although it serves a different purpose than the mere promotion of learning. Activities associated with *formative assessment* (Assessment *for* Learning) do not result in an evaluation. Both, the teacher and the learner, to determine where learners are in their learning and how to achieve learning goals, use information about what a student knows, understands, and is able to do.

"When the cook tastes the soup, that's formative. When the guests taste the soup, that's summative."

Stake, R. cited in Earl, L. 2004. *Assessment As Learning: Using classroom achievement to Maximize Student Learning.* Experts in Assessment. Corwin Press Inc. Thousand Oaks, California.

Thomas A. Angelo and K. Patricia Cross in their 1993 research on Classroom Assessment Techniques have identified a number of classroom strategies that are particularly effective in promoting formative assessment practice:

> Questioning is used not only as a pedagogical tool but also as a deliberate way for the teacher to find out what students know, understand, and are able to do.

> Effective teacher feedback, which focuses on established success criteria and tells the students what they have achieved and where they need to improve.

> Peer feedback, which occurs when a student uses established success criteria to tell another student what they have achieved and where improvement is necessary.

> Student self-assessment against success criteria, which encourages students to take responsibility for their own learning.

What is Assessment as Learning?

The graphic below designed by the Australian state of Victoria helps visualize assessment as a formula to be applied. That formula purports that to be comprehensive the assessment cycle must include instances in which the teacher drives the collection of data on the students as the training event unravels, instances in which students drive the collection of data on their own progress as the training unravels, and an instance in which the teacher gathers conclusive data to evaluate the class, students' performance, as well as the impact of the instruction.

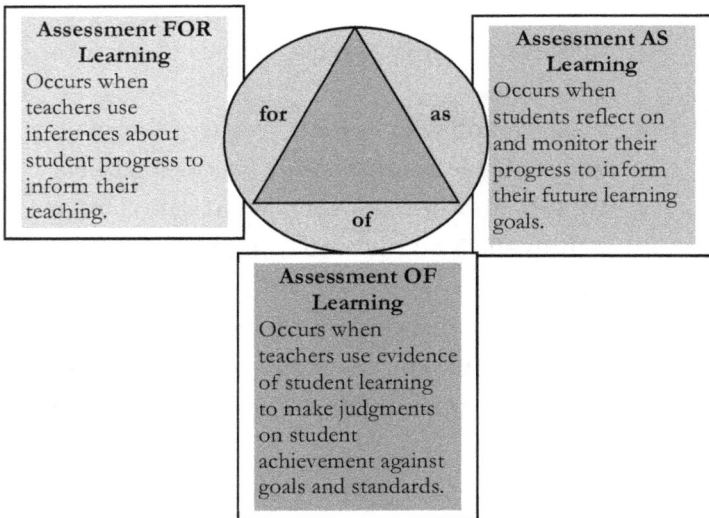

Assessment FOR Learning
Occurs when teachers use inferences about student progress to inform their teaching.

for

as

of

Assessment AS Learning
Occurs when students reflect on and monitor their progress to inform their future learning goals.

Assessment OF Learning
Occurs when teachers use evidence of student learning to make judgments on student achievement against goals and standards.

State of Victoria (Department of Education and Early Childhood Development), 2007.

"Assessment for Learning is the process of seeking and interpreting evidence for use by learners and their teachers to decide where the learners are in their learning, where they need to go and how best to get there."

Assessment Reform Group (UK 2002)

Assessment *for learning* contributes to the development of effective learning programs. If assessments *of learning* provide evidence of achievement for public reporting, then assessments *for learning* serve to help students learn more and learn better. The crucial distinction is between assessment to determine the status of learning and assessment to promote greater learning.

Stiggins, R. J. 2002. Assessment Crisis: The Absence of Assessment FOR Learning, in *Phi Delta Kappan* Vol.83, No.10 pp758-765.

Assessment for learning, also known as formative assessment, is used during instruction by the teacher to see how students are learning based on the instructional approach being used and to meet students' learning needs. How can we develop student ownership of content, increase motivation, and engagement through assessment? If formative assessment is to be effective, learners must be trained in self-assessment so they can not only fully understand the main purposes of their learning, but also, so they can become independent of the instructor.

Teachers need to answer the following key questions as they interpret information gleaned from assessments:

> To what extent are students achieving the standards?
> Where are the strengths and gaps in student understanding of concepts?
> Are students increasing their ability to solve problems and apply knowledge?
> How well is the program meeting the needs of all students?

Assessment as learning is a type of formative assessment that makes all the difference to student learning; one that we should strive to become comfortable with; one that is controlled and designed by the students, for the benefit of the students; and is responsible for driving students to higher degrees of autonomy and engagement. Assessment as learning is used during instruction to build metacognition and motivation in students by meaningfully involving them in the assessment process as designers, assessors and consumers. Assessment as learning is the ultimate goal, where students become their own best assessors, which indicates that they have fully internalized the learning goals, the standards, and are fully capable of monitoring their own progress toward higher levels of learning. When assessment as learning becomes ipsative, comparison with others becomes irrelevant. The critical reference point becomes the student's own prior work, aspirations, and targets for continued learning. Assessment as learning should culminate in ipsative assessment. Ipsative assessment is the practice of assessing present performance against the prior performance of the person being assessed. Rubrics and checklists go a long way in helping learners get there. The ultimate user of assessment information elicited in order to improve learning is the student.

Principles to guide assessment practices

1. Students are the KEY assessment users.

2. A balance of assessment FOR and OF learning should be used.

3. Assessment should be constructive; it should focus on achievement and progress.

4. Assessment and instruction are interdependent.

5. Good quality assessments must be followed by effective feedback.

6. Assessment expectations and curricular outcomes should be communicated clearly to students from the beginning. No guesswork!

7. Meaningful and appropriate assessments should include evidence about student achievement in the areas of content, process, and product.

The primary purpose of assessment is to improve student performance. Good assessment is based on a vision of the kinds of learning we most value for students and how they might best achieve these. It sets out to measure what matters most. Assessment should be based on an understanding of how students learn. Assessment should be an integral component of course design and not something to add afterwards. Good assessment requires clarity of purpose, goals, standards, and criteria. Assessment works best when it is based on clear statements of purpose and goals for the course, the standards which students are expected to achieve, and the criteria against which we measure success. Assessment criteria need to be understandable and explicit, so students know exactly what is expected of them. Assessment methods should be valid, reliable, and consistent. Only assessment instruments and processes that directly measure specifically what they are intended to measure need be selected.

Good assessment requires variety. A single assessment instrument will not tell all we need to know about student achievement and how it can be improved. The use of multiple assessment instruments is preferable to the use of only one. No single assessment works well in all situations and for all purposes. No one assessment can give a clear picture of student achievement. Each type of assessment has its own strengths and weaknesses. Each type of assessment provides a different type of evidence about what students know and can do. Authentic assessment always provides a direct measure of learning. For example, rather than have a student explain how to use a device, authenticity calls for the same student to demonstrate the use of that device. That demonstration would provide a direct measure of learning through true-to-life authentic assessment.

It is important to decide what assessment results mean, what their implications are, and what changes or other decisions should be made. Educators should be careful when interpreting assessment results to avoid implying that they represent broader content or skill areas than the assessment actually measured. Assessment interpretation and use will be improved if based on multiple sources of information.

The ICE Approach

The ICE approach is a framework for assessing learning growth. ICE represents the three stages of learning: Ideas, Connections, and Extensions. It is an innovative approach to assessment developed by two members of Queen's University's Faculty of Education, Sue Fostaty Young and Robert J. Wilson. The authors of this approach show how to recognize these stages of learning development—from a state of beginning to one of competence and expertise—and demonstrate how educators can foster that development in their classrooms. No matter what subject or grade level, the ICE approach will provide teachers with the ability to assess and encourage the learning progress. The ICE model helps to identify what students will do with the learning from your course.

The framework helps to clarify the characteristics that indicate where learners are along the learning continuum and, in so doing, enables teachers to make instructional decisions that maximize learning. It is a simple and powerful assessment tool.

ICE Model Definitions

Ideas (or Items)

Ideas represent the building blocks of learning. They can be discrete 'chunks' of information; facts, definitions, vocabulary, or steps in a process. Assessment tasks, which require recall and repetition of information from books or from lectures, will probably get responses at the ideas level.

Connections

Subject connections

Connections at the subject or topic level can be seen when students make appropriate links between ideas (or chunks of information). They can explain a process, or describe a relationship such as cause-and-effect, or show how separate aspects of a topic or concept fit into a 'big picture'.

Personal or broader connections

Connections at this level show that a student is relating new knowledge to what they already know. Connections might be made to other topics or concepts addressed within the program. Other types of connections might be made to the student's personal or professional experiences.

Extensions

Extensions are the re-working of a student's knowledge and understanding to accommodate new ideas, concepts, and connections. That re-working can mark a shift in the student's way of seeing things. Students may be able to use their extended understanding in novel and creative ways. They may make extended connections to very different domains of their knowledge, skills, and experiences. Students can answer *"So what?" questions* – by extrapolating, predicting outcomes or working out implications.

The ICE Approach offers a compact and powerful framework for understanding what learning is and how it is demonstrated.

The ICE Approach proposes that learning takes place at three distinct levels of thinking, which the authors refer to as 'Ideas', 'Connections', and 'Extensions':

Each phase of learning, 'Ideas', 'Connections', and 'Extensions', represents a stage of learning development--movement from novice toward expert, from superficial to deep.

IDEAS are demonstrated when students convey:

The fundamentals

Basic facts

Vocabulary definitions

Details

Elemental concepts

CONNECTIONS are made when students:

Demonstrate the relationship or connection among the basic concepts

Demonstrate a relationship or connection between what was learned and what they already know

EXTENSIONS are revealed when students:

Use their new learning in novel ways, apart from the initial learning situation

Answer the hypothetical questions: So, what does this mean? How does this shape my view of the world?

The ICE model is not tied to any particular form of assessment (such as rubrics, assignments, or tests) but works with all of them. Nor does it depend on the teacher to be the monitor of learning unless needed or desired. Rather, it is most useful when it is taught to learners, even very young learners, so that they can identify where they are in their learning and will be able then to plot their own next steps. Simply put, the ICE model holds that learning a new concept, a new attitude, or a new skill begins with discrete bits of knowledge. When you are presented with your first digital camera, for example, you begin by trying to discover what each icon means, what all the buttons do, and how the viewfinder works. You may follow the manual point by point to learn how to replace the batteries and how to use the on-screen menu, clicking through one line at a time. These basic learnings are called Ideas in the ICE model and are seen as essential building blocks to all learning.

The required steps become automatic as you play with the camera, and slowly you will discover shortcuts to the step-by-step approach. Combining a timed shot with a dark background becomes possible, and so will overlaying one image on another, for example. This linking of discrete pieces of knowledge occurs almost naturally as we learn, unless we are content with the more routine ways of doing things. In the ICE model, these linkages are called Connections. A variation of this form of connection occurs when you attach old learning (what you remember from your old camera that might still apply) with the new.

Finally, it may happen that your interest in the camera and what it can do moves into a desire to produce your own prints and using them to make cards and invitations. This inclination to take old learning and turn it in a new direction is characteristic of those who are motivated to take their learning deeper. We often see these novel elaborations happen in a hobby, a sport, or in the arts, but they can be encouraged in the classroom as well. In the ICE model, these elaborations are called Extensions.

1. What was your rationale for assessing students?

2. How would you implement assessment As learning?

3. What would it take for you to relinquish some control over the design and administration of student assessment?

Chapter 8

BIAS IN ASSESSMENT

When we integrate assessment throughout our lessons, we stand a better chance of determining and even controlling what our students actually learn. Yet, assessment, despite all its merits, is not without its problems. Bias is one of them.

Assessment bias refers to the qualities of an assessment instrument that offend or unfairly penalize a group of students because of the students' gender, ethnicity, socioeconomic status, religion, or other such group defining characteristics. Biases are aspects of an assessment such as content, language, or examples that might distort the performance of a group – either for better or worse. Two forms of assessment bias are unfair penalization and offensiveness. Offended, angry students may not perform at their best.

The content or construction of an assessment may be biased, giving unfair advantage to one group over another. For example, an assessment of a student's social engagement in class may conclude that a student who does not make eye contact with a teacher is shy or un-engaged, whereas in some cultures it is inappropriate for some people, younger or of the opposite gender, to make eye contact with an authority figure.

The formatting of an assessment tool or the assessor's personality may favor one group of students over another. For example, knowledge checks, which have to be completed within a limited timeframe on a computer, may well penalize students who are not proficient with computers but who may well be proficient in the material being assessed.

Students who are familiar with a certain assessment format may well have learned answering strategies that maximize performance, while students who are unfamiliar with such formats are at a disadvantage.

"Some inherent biases in assessments are unavoidable. Unfortunately, it is not possible to produce a culture-free test." (Berry, 1966; Bloom, 1981).

Culture-fair or culture-free tests have not been very successful at eliminating bias. How can we separate culture from cognition? Do we not acquire information by filtering it through our own experiences, our likes, and dislikes? Ironically, our filters cause biases.

A cognitive bias is the common tendency to acquire and process information by filtering it through one's own likes, dislikes, and experiences. Bias arises from various processes that are sometimes difficult to distinguish. These include information-processing shortcuts (*heuristics*), motivational factors, and social influence. There are numerous types of cognitive biases and more continue to be identified. Here is a list of just a few:

— Selective perception – the tendency for expectations to affect perception.

— Confirmation bias – the tendency to search for or interpret information in a way that confirms one's preconceptions.

— Curse of knowledge – when knowledge of a topic diminishes one's ability to think about it from a less-informed perspective.

— Experimenter's or Expectation bias – the tendency for experimenters to believe, certify, and publish data that agree with their expectations for the outcome of an experiment, and to disbelieve, discard, or downgrade the corresponding weightings for data that appear to conflict with those expectations.

— In-group bias – the tendency for people to give preferential treatment to others they perceive to be members of their own groups.

— Illusory superiority – overestimating one's desirable qualities, and underestimating undesirable qualities relative to other people. (Also known as "Lake Wobegon effect," "better-than- average effect," or "superiority bias").

— Trait ascription bias – the tendency for people to view themselves as relatively variable in terms of personality, behavior, and mood while viewing others as much more predictable.

— Fundamental attribution error is the tendency for people to over-emphasize personality-based explanations for behaviors observed in others while under-emphasizing the role and power of situational influences on the same behavior.

— Ultimate attribution error – similar to the fundamental attribution error, in this error a person is likely to make an internal attribution to an entire group instead of the individuals within the group.

— Status quo bias – the tendency to like things to stay relatively the same.

— Google effect: the tendency to forget information that can be easily found online.

Assessments can give rise to erroneous judgments about learners, their learning, or their progress. This can happen when assessment tools are themselves biased, or when judgments are based on data without sufficient consideration being given to the material's or teacher's potential for bias, when what is assessed has not been taught or the expectations have not been made explicit.

Communication styles and language differences reveal bias in assessment better than any other element. But personal values are the real source of these educational biases, according to professor Gregory J. Cizek and his book, "The Real Testing Bias: The Role of Values In Educational Assessment".

Expectation bias is programmed into us to dislike things or to like things. It is the tendency to see what we expect to see, while requiring more information to recognize something unexpected. Expectation bias makes us overconfident and can make us intolerant toward competing hypotheses. It distorts how we look at and process information. It is the tendency to believe in things that you expect. Not bothering to analyze, measure, or doubt the conclusion you expect or hope for. Our expectations derive from our values.

There may be a tendency to see in students what we expect to see (self-fulfilling prophecy), since the data generated may be biased by teacher expectations. Our mind's eye tends to see what we want it to see.

"Implicit (unconscious) bias and stereotyping are gaining increasing attention as a possible explanation of unequal treatment in a number of settings including education, employment, health care, and law." Dr. James Outtz, an industrial and organizational psychologist, explains that scientists define unconscious bias as implicit attitudes, actions, or judgments that are controlled by automatic evaluation without a person's awareness. Existing research shows that we all engage in a cognitive process called "categorization" to simplify and streamline how we perceive others (e.g. sex, race, or age). This process can lead to stereotype application that influences our thoughts and behaviors towards members of certain groups.

The teacher-student relationship, among a number of social power relationships is one significant example in which the application of stereotypes and biases may be particularly detrimental to members of minority groups or more generally, underrepresented groups. Teacher expectations influence teacher behavior, which in turn significantly influences student learning and achievement. In the classroom, teacher unconscious biases may negatively impact student achievement. Available research, however, indicates that unconscious bias may be reversed once brought to a person's attention.

Bias is unavoidable; but it can be mitigated. Awareness is the modality of its mitigation. To mitigate bias as much as possible some of the keys in assessing students are:

— To involve them as contributors in the development and design of their own assessment: student-involved assessment, and/or assessment as learning;

— To have students conduct peer assessments and self-assessment, a valuable process for enhancing student critical thinking skills and improving learning performance.

— To help students develop their metacognitive skills;

— Use authentic assessments (portfolios, etc.)

— Have students teach the class or teach-back.

Someone else chooses what students study. Someone else determines the terms of the engagement. What would happen if students themselves were to define their learning interests and priorities, and determine the terms of the engagement? Would they have more control over the outcome?

Failure is a social construct. It is a negative frame or judgment usually placed on someone else. It is not an aberration. According to sociologist Pierre Bourdieu, education supports and reproduces the social order, the status quo. It does not necessarily empower or liberate, as it should. The reproduction of structures of domination in society depends on the imposition of cultural values which are presented as universal but whose content and context are politically and historically determined – and therefore arbitrary.

Unless they have abdicated their mission, educators are change agents by vocation and avocation. When they push conformity, they sell out and kill the possibilities. It is when they cultivate difference, divergent thinking, diverse perspectives, and creative abrasion that they honor their mandate. Difference generates change. Promoting learning is an educator's characteristic contribution to the creation of the future, and how educators help us resist fatalism. Educators exist to help people become more fully who they are, cultivate their unique talents and self-actualize. They exist to bring to light opportunities, to serve as role models and leaders when few are available; to lavish praise and encouragements, neutralize the effects of discouragement and ridicule, and provide the skills and substance for the dream of a better tomorrow to become a reality. To become who we are, we all benefit from help and guidance. Educators are ideally situated to lead transformational change.

Here are some Classroom Assessment Techniques (CATs) that mitigate bias and enable immediate course corrections. During breaks teachers read students' anonymous responses to specific CAT questions and address them after the break. That way, they are able to intervene and correct misunderstandings while training is still in session and there is still time.

Source: Classroom Assessment Techniques), by Thomas A. Angelo and K. Patricia Cross (1993)

Name	Description	What to do with data	Time Required
Background Knowledge Probe	This CAT collects specific and useful data on students' prior learning. Prepare two or three open-ended questions or multiple choices that probes students' knowledge of subject. Hand out at first meeting or direct students' to answer.	After they answer, collect the response, collect and rate. Alternate: Have students work in pairs or small groups to come up with answers.	Medium
Focused Listing	A tool to determine what learners recall as the most important point of a topic. Select an important topic or concept that the class has just studied and describe it in a word or brief phrase. Write the word at the top of a sheet of paper. Set a time limit	Compare students' lists with your list. Categorize students' responses into "related" and "unrelated". Categorize responses according to the type or degree of relationship they have to the focus topic.	Low

	(2-3 minutes) and make a list of important words and phrases you can recall that are related to the heading. Give students a time limit and have them respond.		
Misconception/ Preconception	Assesses students' 'prior knowledge and focuses on uncovering prior knowledge that may hinder or block further learning. Consider a topic around which there may be misconceptions. Create a simple questionnaire to elicit information. Explain reasons for using this CAT to students.	Group results into 4 categories; those that elicit strong reactions at 'correct' and 'incorrect' ends of scales, those that elicit mostly incorrect or mostly correct and those that students are unsure of.	Medium

Empty Outlines	Helps faculty find out how well the students have caught the important points of a lecture or other presentation. Let students know how much they will have to complete and how much time they have.	Compare their responses with what was expected or look at range of responses.	Medium
Memory Matrix	Assess students' recall of important course content and their skill at quickly organizing information into categories provided by the instructor. Draw a matrix with row and column matrix and empty spaces. Direct student to fill in blanks.	Tally frequency of correct cells and look for differences, between and among cells. Assess correctness.	Medium

Minute Paper	During last few minutes of class, ask students to answer on a half sheet of paper: "What was the most important point you learned today?" and "What point remains least clear to you?" The purpose is to elicit data about student's comprehension of a particular class session.	Review responses and note any useful comments. During the next class time, emphasize the issues illuminated by your students' comments	Low
Muddiest Point	Ask students to jot down a quick response to ": What was the muddiest point in...?"	Look through responses and sort them into piles—groups of like 'muddiest points'. Discuss with students	Low
Categorizing Grid	Helps to discover how well students understand 'what goes with what'. It prompts students to make explicit the implicit rules they are using to categorize information.	Check the grids to see whether students placed the right items in the correct boxes. Look for patterns in incorrect data	Low

Defining Features Matrix	Assess students' skill at categorizing important information according to a given set of critical defining features. Best in courses that require students to distinguish between closely related or seemingly similar items or concepts.	Compare students' matrices with master copy. See if students are paying attention to certain features as opposed to others.	Medium
Pro and Con Grid	Gives faculty a quick overview of a class's analysis of the pros and cons, cost and benefits, or advantages or disadvantages of an issue of mutual concern. Focus on a decision, judgment, etc. or issue. Write out a prompt that will elicit thoughtful pros and cons.	Compare students' grids with yours. Determine what they omitted or included. Give the class group feedback.	Low

Content, From, and Function Outline	Designed to elicit information on the students' skills at separating and analyzing the informational contents, form and function of writing. It is also called the "What, How and Why" Outlines	A simple way to assess the class' understanding is to keep a running tally of the problem spots in the test and the questions most difficult to answer.	Medium-High
Analytic memos	It is a simulation exercise that requires students to write a one-two page analysis of a specific problem or issue. Assesses student's ability to analyze assigned problems and their skills at communicating in a clear and concise manner	Devise a checklist of 3 to 5 major points to look for in each memo and read each memo to check for theses points. Limit yourself to brief comments.	High

One sentence Summary	Students summarize knowledge of a topic by constructing a single sentence that answers the questions, "Who does what to whom, when, where, how and why?" The purpose is to select only the defining features of an idea.	Evaluate the quality of each summary quickly and holistically. Note whether students have identified the essential concepts of the class topic and their interrelationships. Share your observations with your student's	Low-medium
Invented Dialogues	This provides information on students' ability to capture the essence of the personalities of others. Students synthesize their knowledge of issues, personalities and historical periods into the form of a structured dialogue.	Look for the number of important points addressed in the dialogue and rate the quality of reasoning.	High
What is the Principle?	This will assess students' ability to associate specific problems with	Tally the number of right and wrong answers and note patterns in specific wrong answers given.	Low-Medium

	the general principles used to solve them. This provides students with a few problems and asks them to state the principle that best applies to each problem.		
Documented Problem Solutions	This CAT aims to assess how students solve problems and assess how well students understand and describe their problem-solving methods. This prompts students to keep track of the steps they take in solving a problem and show and tell how they worked it out.	Select some responses to analyze and pick three responses in which answers are correct and solutions well documented. Compare with those that are well documented but not correct. Note what led to successful outcomes and what didn't.	Low-High

Directed Paraphrasing	Ask students to write a layman's' translation of something they just learned—geared to a specific individual or audience—to assess their ability to comprehend and transfer concepts.	Categorize student responses according to characteristics you feel are important. Analyze the responses both within and across categories, noting ways you could address student needs.	Low-Medium
Applications Cards	After teaching about an important theory, principle or procedure, ask students to write down at least one real-world application for what they have just learned to determine how well they can transfer to their learning.	Quickly read once through the applications and categorize them according to their quality. Pick out a broad range of examples and present tem to the class.	Low-Medium

Student Generated Test Questions	Allow students to write test questions and model answers for specified topics in a format consistent with course exams. This will give students the opportunity to evaluate the course topics, reflect on what they understand, and what good test items are.	Make a rough tally of the questions your students propose and the topics they cover. Evaluate the questions and use the good ones for discussion. You may also want to revise the questions and use them on the upcoming exam.	Med-High
Classroom Opinion Polls	The purpose is to discover student opinions about course-related issues. This technique builds on informal class polling, providing more anonymity for students.	Count and tally.	Low
Goal Ranking and Matching	The primary purpose is to assess the students' 'degree of fit' between students' learning goals and instructor goals. Students	This technique should be used in the first week of class so instructors can see what students hope to get from the class.	Low to Medium

	list a few learning goals they hope to achieve through the course and rank the relative importance of the goals.		
Self-Assessment of Ways of Learning	This technique provides instructors with a simple way to assess students' learning styles or preference for learning. It prompts students to describe their general approaches to learning by comparing themselves with several different profiles and choosing one that most closely resembles them.	This is relatively difficult to construct, but easy to analyze. Tally the number of students who choose each style. Then tally the answers to related questions and summarize the responses for class discussion.	Low to High

Punctuated Lectures	This technique is designed to provide immediate, on the spot feedback on how students are learning from a lecture or demonstration. It requires students to go through 5 steps: listen, stop, reflect, write and give feedback.	Analyze student comments with the goal of helping them develop their skills at monitoring their own listening.	Low
Chain Notes	Students pass around an envelope on which the teacher has written one question about the class. When the envelope reaches a student s/he spends a moment to respond to the question and then places the response in the envelope.	Go through the student responses and determine the best criteria for categorizing the data with the goal of detecting response patterns. Discuss the patterns of responses with students, which can lead to better teaching and learning.	Low
Group Instructional Feedback Technique	This provides instructors with a quick, rough summary of the most frequent	Tally the most common responses, particularly the suggestions. List comments. Give	Medium

	responses to three questions: 1) What do students think is helping them learn? 2) What is hindering their learning? 3) What specific suggestions do they have for improving learning in the classroom?	students feedback on the three most common responses.	
Classroom Assessment Quality Circles	This involves students in structured and ongoing assessment of course materials, activates and assignments for two reasons: 1) provide a vehicle for regularly collecting responses from students on the course and 2) offer students a structured, positive way to become more actively involved in their classroom learning.	When meeting with quality circles, listen carefully, ask questions and talk little. Look for patterns over time.	High

Group Work Evaluations	These are simple questionnaires used to collect feedback on students' reactions to cooperative learning where students work in cooperative learning. They help students and instructors see what is going well and what is not in learning groups.	Tally the fixed-response answers and results across groups. Look at feedback for indications some groups are working well or poorly.	Low

1. What assumptions if surfaced and discussed would improve learning in your classroom?

2. What steps can you take to minimize the effects of bias in your training?

3. What biases are built in the materials and the approach you use to deliver content?

Chapter 9

FEEDBACK FOR LEARNING

Giving Effective Feedback for Learning

Feedback is used to help students stay on track so they can achieve their ultimate goal. Without feedback, mistakes go uncorrected, good practices are not reinforced; competence is achieved haphazardly or not at all. The intent is to help students assess their performance; identify areas where they are right on target and provide them with tips on what they can do next to improve areas that need correcting. Through feedback, we try to develop a plan of action and set goals for future student performance.

Feedback is not evaluation. Evaluative feedback is often experienced as a judgment about a person's worth or goodness. We do not seek to assign value, but to understand, and to either redirect or encourage behavior. Unlike evaluation, which judges performance, feedback is part of the process of helping students assess their own performance. To that end, being descriptive in reflecting on what actually happened is more helpful than simply deciding if it was right or wrong. Evaluative language is avoided.

If an evaluation has to be made for any legitimate reason, remember, there is a big difference between judging a person and judging their actions. A personal evaluation is often perceived as a judgment of the whole person and accepted as implying that there is an unchangeable attribute. A behavioral evaluation judges the action of a person, but not the person. This makes negative evaluation easier for the other person to accept. When practicing behavioral evaluations in the guise of feedback for learning few people are skilled at making others feel supported and truly seen. We prefer to never use feedback as evaluation but rather as an opportunity to discuss observations and tentatively check our interpretations.

With interpretive checks, you seek to test your understanding of what has been said by interpreting and paraphrasing back to the other person what you think has been said. This is typically followed by a question to allow the other person to agree with your interpretation or offer a correction.

-- *Is this right?*

Understanding is not perfect and testing understanding is generally a very good thing to do. It is generally flattering too, as you are showing active interest in what your interlocutor is saying.

Feedback must go both ways. The person giving it must also receive it and the person receiving it must also give it, especially if doing so facilitates its reception. Learning is a cooperative effort between student and instructor. Both contribute to the dynamic at play; both have needs that must be met in that teacher/student relationship.

Types of Feedback

Silence

The absence of feedback or response is also feedback. It maintains the status quo, and may even make things worse by decreasing confidence over the long-term, reducing performance, and creating surprises during performance appraisals.

Negative Criticism

It identifies behaviors or results that are undesirable and not up to standard. It intends to stop undesirable behaviors; however, it generates excuses and/or blame, decreases confidence, leads to avoidance, and hurts relationships.

Informative co-exploration

It identifies behaviors that are highly regarded and specifies how to incorporate them in the future. It intends to shape or change behavior to improve performance, *and* improves confidence and relationships in the process.

Example: "Let's discuss what happens when the assignment is completed on time and the effect that has on others. Let us discuss ways to make certain it is done on time."

Positive Reinforcement

It identifies behaviors that are desired, that are up to or exceeding standards. It intends to increase desired performance, and results in increased confidence, improved performance, and increased motivation.

Example: "I appreciate how well you prepare your articles! There was no error in your delivery. Thanks!"

Probing

Probing seeks to find more information by asking deeper questions that seek specific information. You are seeking to understand not just what is said, but the whole person underneath.

Could you tell me more about what happened?

The Sandwich approach to feedback

Positive feedback /negative feedback / positive feedback

This "sandwich approach" makes sense conceptually – by putting the negative feedback in the middle – others will likely be more open to it. Mainly because they have heard something positive first and last, the relationship should be maintained, even if the negative comments in the middle can be pretty hard to hear. This approach can work but is often ineffective. It sounds fake. Too often the intent of the sandwiched feedback was not to make balanced comments at all, but only to make the negative feedback more palatable. The fact that it is so formulaic makes it hard to convey sincerity, honesty and genuineness.

To be effective feedback should be specific, not general. It should be timely. It should focus on a specific behavior rather than the individual or her intentions. It should go both ways and involve openly sharing information and observations back and forth. It should encourage self-assessment. It should be as consistent as possible, not contradictory. It should be sincere and honest, and contain no mixed messages, no 'however' or 'but.' It should be easy to understand, and deliver the message as simply as possible; and should culminate in a plan of action. Students identify the areas for improvement and the manner of the improvement and, jointly with the teacher, develop a solution. Students must maintain ownership of their development.

Student self-regulation can lead to students seeking, accepting, and acting on feedback information—or not. Effective learners create internal routines that include figuring out when they need more information, or an assessment or suggestions, and strategies for getting this feedback. Students are more willing to expend efforts in getting and dealing with feedback if they have confidence in themselves as learners, a sense of self-efficacy, and confidence that the information will be useful and thus worth the effort.

Choose your words carefully before providing feedback. Feedback must be positive to be constructive. Being "positive" does not mean being artificially happy or saying work is good when it is not. Being positive means describing how the strengths in a student's work match the criteria for good work and how those strengths show what the student is learning. Being positive means pointing out where improvement is needed and suggesting things the student could do about it. Just noticing what is wrong without offering suggestions to make it right is not helpful. The learning conversation must move from a focus on the past – feedback, to a focus on future actions – feedforward, to use a phrase coined by executive coach Marshall Goldsmith.

Next, feedback should address the current performance in relation to a previous plan of action derived from the previous feedback session. Feedback should not be an event, but a process.

A Tool for Giving Effective Feedback: DASH

Describe

Do	Don't
Describe the other person's behavior objectively Use concrete terms Describe a specific time, place, action Describe the behavior not the "motive"	Let your emotional reaction drive the conversation Use abstract, vague terms Generalize for all time Guess motives or goals

Acknowledge

Do	Don't
Acknowledge your concerns Express them calmly State concerns as related to goals Describe the impact of the behavior	Unleash emotional outbursts State feelings negatively, making a put-down or attack Attack the person's character

Specify

Do	Don't
Specify the concrete actions you want stopped or performed Ask for a change in behavior Be realistic in your requests for change Specify or ask how you can help	Merely imply you'd like a change Ask for too large or too small a change Ask for changes in traits or qualities Assume that responsibility for the change lies solely with the employee

Hearten

Do	Don't
Reaffirm the other's ability to make the change End on a positive note	Express doubts about the person's ability to make the change

Source: MIT Performance Development
http://hrweb.mit.edu/performance/

1. How frequently are you able to provide learning feedback to students?

2. What difference do you wish your feedback would make?

3. How could you ensure that your feedback is well received?

Chapter 10

FROM TEACHING TO LEADERSHIP

Teaching is an act of influence. Acts of influence seek to affect the thoughts, behavior, and feelings of other people. Students allow teachers to lead them by acknowledging their authority − their right − to influence them. Students are the source of a teacher's power. That teacher power is a function of their relationship.

To truly become transformational, teaching must inspire others and engage their emotions. Logical persuasion alone will fall short of inspiring others. Teachers must seek to connect at a deeper level. They must connect with what drives people and gives meaning to their lives.

"Teaching is at the heart of leading. In fact, it is through teaching that leaders lead others... teaching is how ideas and values get transmitted. Therefore, in order to be a leader at any level of an organization, a person must be a teacher. Simply put, if you aren't teaching, you aren't leading."

Noel Tichy: "The Leadership Engine."

To teach is to lead. An effective teacher can lead without the benefit of fancy titles or other accouterments of power. He or she leverages almost exclusively the personal sources of power and influence – knowledge, familiarity, attraction, character and expressiveness, and the most powerful source of all, willpower. A teacher starts with the end in mind, and articulates a powerful vision of what can be. A teacher provides all necessary information. He or she assigns tasks, harnesses peer pressure; gives individualized attention to stakeholders in the classroom, and seeks their input. He or she intervenes when necessary; monitors engagement and productivity and takes responsibility for the outcome of his or her efforts. The teacher is in charge of the student-centered classroom.

It bears repeating that some of the factors that limit a teacher's personal power are: *"lack of self-confidence, fear of embarrassment, low expectations of others, the need to be perfect, lack of enthusiasm, wanting to be liked, closed-mindedness, being controlling, lack of trust* [in students], *being overly critical, the fear of taking risks, the fear of failure, indecisiveness, low self-worth, and focusing on problems."*

A teacher must secure buy-in, get commitment, move students enough so they want to spread their newfound insights to others, and inspire leadership. To be more effective, teachers must know who they are, take a stand, step up, stand in their power, and give themselves away generously if they are to become compelling change agents. A teacher's personal power starts when he or she knows her subject matter thoroughly, can articulate it to anyone, simplifying or making it more complex as the context requires. A teacher's personal power also increases when she is willing to exercise her willpower for the benefit of the students.

Some of the factors that always bolster a teacher's personal power are the use of a compelling tone of voice, focused listening, energy, enthusiasm, self-confidence, genuine interest in others, approachability, rapport-building, trust, supportive behaviors, encouragements, persistence, and the ability to be vulnerable.

A teacher's personal power increases even more with the articulation of a powerful vision of the future – when the teacher provides the big picture. A vision that provides a compelling answer to the question '*why*' (is it important for us to learn this) and states a higher purpose that builds on what students care about. The goal here is to have students step up and show up for themselves because they want to believe in the possibilities.

Students, like all people, look for meaning and purpose in their lives. Like all people, they value fun, that state of flow driven by activity that engrosses all their attention in the here and now. Students value power, that ability to choose moment by moment. Students value freedom, autonomy and self-direction. Like all people, students value belonging, the sense of acceptance one derives from being connected to others. To the extent a teacher manipulates the environment well enough to meet these needs, and provided the most basic survival needs of students have been met, little remains in the way of learning.

Expectations are emotional reactions. They predict nothing with any level of accuracy. In and of themselves, unexpressed, and not acted upon, they have no power. Expectations are a form of bias, and a powerful tool in transformation. Whether positive or negative, they are a choice. It is when expectations are stated, publicized and acted upon that their full effect gets felt. Expectations tell us more about the people who hold them than they tell us about the people they are directed to. Expectations are the switch of our motivation. They tell us about the mindset of those who expect, whether they are generous in their view of others, enabling, facilitative, or closed, narrow, and invalidating. Invalidation occurs when the spoken and unspoken messages our students receive cause them to feel inadequate, and threaten their ability to learn.

In so many invisible ways, expectations mold each student's experience in any given classroom, moment to moment. Teachers are more patient with students they believe in. Teachers give more attention, explanations, opportunities to shine, support, actionable and specific feedback, smiles, and other signs of approval and validation to the students they "expect" to succeed. Why not make a conscious effort to ensure that all students receive reinforcing cues that prod them along the way to the success they are all truly capable of.

A teacher's job requires that he or she unconditionally express faith in the capacity for growth of the people he works with, no matter their current level of development. Students should leave the learning experience enhanced, not diminished. To not strategically hold high expectations of them is to sabotage their learning. To leverage the power of expectation, a teacher must be sincere in becoming Pollyannaish.

To teach is to lead a transformation. If you expect consistent, across the board performance beyond expectations from people, how do you prime the pump?

When you think of a mushroom, what comes to mind?

If you answered 'fungus' and 'dirt,' you are right!

Where do mushrooms grow?

Certainly not in direct sunlight, right? Yes, in darker, moist or humid places. They thrive on manure. Fungi have an important role in the decomposition of organic matter. Along with bacteria, they are the major decomposers in most ecosystems.

What does the expression mushroom management conjure up in your mind?

Traci Kidder in "The Soul of a New Machine" coined this expression. It is an allusion to a way of relating in which people are treated like mushrooms by their leadership. They are kept in the dark, covered with dung, and when they grow too big, are canned. Leaders make decisions about people, (those affected by those decisions), without consulting them.

Mushroom learning managers hoard information and in so doing encourage rumormongering and fear. A few people are singled out for attention, and get offered opportunities for growth; that in turn leads to the development of an 'in' crowd, cliques, stovepipes and silos. The pecking order is clearly defined. Other people plow along aimlessly, dispirited, not understanding where they fit in the larger picture and what their own prospects are. They become increasingly fearful of teachers and focused on avoiding negative attention and mistakes.

Showing like-mindedness, being agreeable and fitting-in become absolute imperatives for survival. People grow fearful of asking questions, of expressing dissent and alternate viewpoints. As a result, distrust sets in, muted cynicism prevails, engagement goes down, and absenteeism increases.

Mushroom managers and the teachers that act like them are often more concerned with their own advancement and less concerned with advocating for their people. Mushroom learning managers rely on a lot of poor assumptions about what people know and what motivates them. What students know for a fact is that the teachers do not care about them or the institution. Learning suffers. They communicate when they have to, and talk at you. Listening makes them feel less powerful, so they avoid it.

They mobilize no one behind a vision, and produce no positive change. So, what can the teachers that act like that typically expect of their students in terms of day-to-day performance?

What level of performance are they priming the pump for?

They seldom ask powerful questions. These questions produce insight, unsettle the status quo, and create more work. Their sense of control is easily shaken. They are mostly quality controllers, enforcers, judges and/or gatekeepers. In the rush to get things done, they tolerate little to no deviations from standard operating procedures. They have answers, or feel they ought to have answers. New possibilities create anxiety, (exactly what they cannot afford more of).

If you expect consistent, across the board performance beyond expectations from people, how do you prime the pump? What do you do differently?

Do you not encourage constructive conflict? The exclusion of conflict carries a heavy price. Conflict is the creative force in the world that gives birth to real exploration and change. Do you not encourage the free flow of communication? Do you not encourage large-scale information sharing? Do you not encourage decentralized decision-making? Do you not encourage all manner of open collaboration? What about a bottom-up approach to organizing the work, decision-making and initiatives? Do you not actively promote a culture of inquiry? Do you not unleash students' genius? Transformational teachers do!

Questions instigate out of the box thinking and are the engines of profound transformations. Communication confronts us with limits to our perceptions, our interpretations, and our evaluations, and provides impetus for discovery. Communication is all about access. Access drives inclusion. Inclusion creates intersections. Intersections provoke new and better ideas.

True leadership is not value-neutral. It is value-laden. The power of values is mobilizing and compelling. Transformational teachers use the absolute most effective influence approach and techniques known to men, an inspirational approach through an appeal to values and modeling. An appeal to values is truly an appeal to the heart. Transformational teachers seek others' commitment and leadership, not just their compliance.

A leader's job is to embrace conflict and the cacophony of ideas that comes with it, harness conflict and give it a future focus, keeping it strategic. A leader's job is to connect with people by empowering them; granting them more authority, more support, more resources, more freedom and more confidence. A true leader's job is to get over himself and give away his power generously. A true leader's job is to make leaders out of all those that follow. That is what drives engagement and results.

To become more transformational, we can start by adopting a different stance. We can invest in getting the people whose self-image is wrapped up in being people who know the answers, to become people who know the right questions. A big challenge is to get them to relinquish their power to enable others to find their own solutions.

Adopting a different stance as a way of becoming more transformational also involves looking at problem solving in a whole different way. Instead of focusing on problems, we can focus on what invigorates people. We can focus our attention on their positive core, and what is already working. That focus is generative. It produces performance beyond expectations. Becoming more transformational begins when we adopt an inclusive and positive stance. The next step in the journey consists in understanding four components that facilitate transformation.

Intellectual Stimulation

Transformational teachers challenge people to be innovative and creative. The brain is our main productivity tool. Thinking has become the main competency, and there can be no definitive failure in thought. Productive failure results from people actively stretching their thinking to reach higher levels of performance. Transformational teachers nurture and further develop people who think independently and differently.

Individualized Consideration

Transformational teachers demonstrate genuine interest in the needs and concerns of people in ways that are concrete. They meet people face to face to listen exclusively and understand their thought processes. That face-to-face encounter and personal attention is to a great extent responsible for bringing out others' best efforts, and their renewed connection to purpose. Transformational teachers provide opportunities for coaching, mentoring, teaching, and counseling that further reinforce the bonds between the leader and the led. Real power emerges from people wanting to work and learn with you because of the way you interact with them and make them feel. Transformational teachers understand that it is their responsibility to create an environment in which people feel free to talk to them. That realization drives inclusion.

Idealized Influence

True leadership is never an act of control, coercion, or dominance; it is an act of influence. Authentic leaders do not seek to compel. They seek to inspire. They do not impose their will on others; instead, they live according to core beliefs and principles that attract others. Those leaders serve as role models, they "walk the talk," and exemplify highly ethical behavior before gaining respect and trust. Of all the influence techniques in effective leaders' toolboxes, the most significant factor in successfully leveraging Idealized Influence remains willpower, the will to influence, or the courage to act.

Inspirational Motivation

It is not enough for transformational teachers to "walk the talk," and exemplify ethical behavior, they also need to challenge the rest of us to do the same. Transformational agents provide meaning for the task at hand, bolstering our sense of purpose. Purpose and meaning then drive us forward. Transformational teachers appeal primarily to our need for self-realization, or personal growth and self-fulfillment, and at the same time satisfy their personal need for transcendence, or helping others self-actualize.

Transformational teachers make leaders of all their charges.

"*Education either functions as an instrument which is used to facilitate integration of the younger generation into the logic of the present system and bring about conformity or it becomes the practice of freedom, the means by which men and women deal critically and creatively with reality and discover how to participate in the transformation of their world.*"

Paulo Freire, *Pedagogy of the Oppressed*

Bibliography

Christophe, Michel. *The Unraveling. A Leadership Tale.* Leesburg, VA: ProficiencyPlus, 2016.

———. *Le Conservatisme Noir Américain.* 3rd ed. Leesburg, VA: ProficiencyPlus, 2016.

———. *Deux semaines en janvier.* Leesburg, VA: ProficiencyPlus, 2016.

———. *Chronique d'un Noir à la dérive.* Leesburg, VA: ProficiencyPlus, 2016.

www.ingramcontent.com/pod-product-compliance
Lightning Source LLC
Chambersburg PA
CBHW030103070426
42448CB00037B/948